es ist kindergarten nicht

Professional Project Management In Information Technology

M R D A W A L L A C E

PMP, CSM, P2P

ISBN: 1489526994

ISBN 13: 978-1489526991

Library of Congress Control Number: 2013921971

CreateSpace Independent Publishing Platform

North Charleston, South Carolina

CONTENTS

FORMAL BITS

This book is in editorial form and should be considered as a "lessons learnt" report for those of us with a PMI bent (or Lesson Report for those PRINCE2 practitioners) from my time as a PM in IT.

Although I am associated with and strongly support the Project Management Institute via my PMP certification, the OCG via my P2P certification, and the SCRUM Alliance via my CSM certification, the views expressed within this book are my own and not necessarily those of the groups I am associated with.

Please note that the terms "project manager" and "project management" apply to all facets of it and should be interchangeable—within context—of "programme management" and even "portfolio management."

AUTHOR'S NOTE

This book is a series of blogs, essays, and presentations that I should have been writing and giving over the last few years of my career. But I didn't. Due to other commitments (mostly my commitment to laziness), a sabbatical in which two hobbies became quasi professions, two major earthquakes, and a dog eating the first edition of this book, I simply didn't get around to putting the ideas down; I confess to completing "satisficing" (if legitimate) ways of earning my PDUs (professional development units) for the Project Management Institute (PMI) Project Management Practitioner (PMP) credential I hold.

Having recently reentered the profession of project management in the IT (information technology) industry full time (after this bout of unending excuses...I mean...other commitments), I found the profession in a worse state than when I left.

That was a seriously saddening, frustrating, and demoralizing experience. Frankly, I saw project managers in pain. The stress in their lives was unbelievable. I saw people exhibiting the lowest level of human behaviors towards others and a lot of other good people chasing their tails, hiding their mistakes, taking on rubbish processes, feeling down, giving up on themselves, not having the skills and knowledge to complete their jobs, and generally being miserable.

I couldn't believe it. A year after returning I thought about giving up the profession and doing something like running a shop somewhere quiet (seriously!).

However, the mentors and peers that I trust and respect (some of the best PMs in the profession), pulled me out of my malaise to the point where I could hear one of their suggestions: "write a book." They said that at the very least it would allow me to vent, and if I didn't use too many expletives I would probably still be hirable upon publication.

So here it is.

BACKGROUND AND INTRODUCTION

Well I'm not a martyr, I'm not a prophet
And I won't preach to you, But heres a caution
You better understand, That I won't hold your hand
But if it helps you mend, Then I won't stop it
Go on and save yourself, And take it out on me
Audioslave: Cochise

In less than a paragraph, I could explain why IT projects fail, and I wouldn't be telling you anything you don't already know. The actual reason is not very nice; its ugliness is why this is the twelfth version of this book—not edition, but version. The first eleven versions will not see the light of day. They were full of things that, while perhaps I should not have left unsaid, I definitely needed to express them in a much more polite way as opposed to my frustration-ridden vents.

The reason why IT projects fail is not very complex. It doesn't need a "top ten reasons" report or a billion empirically cross-referenced project management statistics from different sources to form the argument. Nor does it need the support of government project management reviews, which bear the same fruit year after year, to explain causality. Finally, the singular reason IT projects fail does not need the backing of—or, more precisely, branding from—a government group or professional project management organisation to give it a voice in the industry and accurately explain the failure of IT projects.

The reason so many IT projects fail—or, the root cause, "the reason"—gives birth to every "top ten" or empirically discovered or proven "cause" offered by IT project and project management reviewers in the last ten years in the industry. All these "causes" have a common denominator that has not been so much overlooked, but politely, quietly, and socially ignored. It's the elephant in the room—and it's a big elephant. We've left it formally unacknowledged for so long that it's now standing there sweating, squashed up in the board room against the magic whiteboard and just behind the chairman, looking embarrassed with its great grey folds spilling over onto the table, now threatening to knock the EA's water to the floor, as it inflates with each passing year.

The elephant is there at every IT project meeting when issues are being discussed, recoveries are taking place, or where the "bad news" is being disclosed or uncovered—once again. In every recovery report I've ever written and with every recommendation, that white-inked elephant on white paper stares at me from the margins. In every fragment of forensic evidence I've uncovered, Jumbo stares out at me from the contracts, financial systems, PMO and (empty) documentation repositories. And yet I've never written anything about the big fella in a single report. I need to be frank. I'm not the first, and I won't be the last.

This includes a self-flagellating assessment because I'm the kind of person (read idiot) that took the PMI code of ethics and general ethos seriously—who actually considered the achievement of attaining their PMP, and more recently PRINCE2 Practioners (P2P) credential, as a significant achievement in their professional career. I am, as ever, the conflicted and tortured soul of an idealistic realist.

That's why you are reading version twelve. Because through all of the scathing, sarcastic, and satirical commentary of the first eleven versions of this book, it dawned on me that I'd missed something crucial. I'd directed a torrent of criticism at the wrong area. Understand that the eleventh version word count was 45,000, and I'd spent the better half of three months researching and writing the book—so a rewrite using a new approach was not a small thing.

So I said at the beginning that I could express to you why IT projects actually fail in a single paragraph. Well, I've changed my mind. Like a magician revealing a rabbit from a hat, allow me to do it in one word.

Ready?

Drum roll.

People.

That's it. The reason is people. IT projects fail because of people. Not bad processes, risk management, constraints, budgets, or ill-defined scopes. IT projects fail because of people.

Ta-da!

The end...

Or is it?

What kind of people make IT projects fail?

Although there's far more to it than can be expressed in a few sentences, here's the paragraph I promised—the redrafted, sensitive, censored twelfth version of it, explaining exactly (and I use the word *exactly* consciously) what kind of people make IT projects fail.

Good people, generally capable people, and unhappy people not acting that great, who aren't sure what their jobs really are and who know something is missing, without the prerequisite qualifications, skills, and experience to actually fulfill their roles, make IT projects fail; and that unfortunately, in my experience, includes most of us.

I know, I know. I'm a bad person for even thinking it, let alone writing it down, especially as it seems to include you, dear reader. I know we should have left the paragraph for the venting we do over the coffee shop table or around the water cooler. You're probably even thinking that no one will ever hire this guy again—well you should have read the first few versions of this book!

I may have broken all our special secret social rules by writing it down and I know I suck for doing it, but really we know it's true and it's probably time we did something about it.

People are not doing a good job at IT project management. This is not something we didn't know or something I feel the need to establish here in this book by referencing the plethora of published project failure reviews.

Those projects don't fail by themselves and it's not happening "over there". The problem isn't endemic, it's definitive, and it's everywhere.

I've just pointed out the elephant.

What's the Book About?

A theme that kept occurring to me in those earlier versions was the theme of "professional project management" versus (for lack of a better term) "lay project management." The experiences I was referencing were about expectations I had about the skills and experience from my peers in the industry and a lack of these in reality.

The point of this book is to provide a commentary and critique of IT, IT projects, and their management (or lack thereof). It's a call to the industry leaders to acknowledge what is happening. Do not underestimate how bad things are out there in ITPM land relative to other industries from project administrators up to the board. Bad practice is everywhere in IT project management and it breeds further bad practice.

This commentary includes an informal overview of the "typical day in the office" to show what is going wrong, an editorial style draft of thoughts about issues that are supporting the low level of practice, and a section on the basics (practices which seem to make a successful difference) that I'm using to outline the minimum standard and associated understandings I think IT project management needs.

This book is also a needle to the project failure report balloon. While I don't disagree with the immense torrent of findings on what makes our IT projects fail (year after year at the cost of millions of dollars and pounds. So the reports themselves aren't making a significant difference then?), I do disagree that what the industry has identified as the root causes of these failures is nothing but the smoke after the bomb has gone off. When something is as blindly obvious as this particular elephant, the approach to resolve is not to use big words and revert to technocracy. The way to fix a problem like this is to keep it basic by using words less than three syllables, to get down into the mud and apply some common sense.

The reason I'm writing this book is that I'm frustrated and tired. I keep being hired to come and fix projects and to shape new ones that go off the rails as soon as I'm away for five minutes. Then amidst all the chaos I'm expected to calmly explain that yet again the reason for the carnage is that basic project management and supporting practices aren't in place, without dropping people in it.

Also like those of us in IT who like Dilbert comics, I'm just a little bit cynical and lean towards sarcasm—so much so that if I see this elephant standing there during our project, trying to look like a water cooler, I just have to bring peanuts and wait for the questions.

Getting to the Problem: That Mound of Dirt Analogy

Picture a prescribed and finite mound of dirt. Metaphorically our job in project management is simply to shovel the mound of dirt from the place it is in to another prescribed place until the ground beneath the mound of dirt is visible and flat. That's it; that's all the job involves.

Each day I go to my place of work, pick up a shovel, and continue shoveling the dirt from one place to another. It's an easy task, and I don't begrudge it. My job also involves coming to an agreement with other people about what the job is and how to do it, and communicating that agreement to other people (to an extent)!

However, despite me carrying out my job each day, I find that vendors, customers, and peers have shoveled the same dirt back onto the mound. Others have been shoveling the dirt to the wrong places—requiring me to shovel it again. Even some have been shoveling other mounds of dirt (working on other projects) without telling anyone. I also find that some extraordinarily helpful engineers and management have taken dirt from elsewhere and piled it into the mound we're digging (adding more work to a project in an uncontrolled manner). Although the very nature and requirement of the job does not change, I find that all levels of management have been misdirecting vendors, customers, and peers.

I have found that some management—despite agreeing what the job is and having not given out shovels (provided basic project management tools and processes)—wouldn't know what a shovel was if someone came up to them and whacked them in the head with one...and yes, it has crossed my mind.

Further, I find peers, assigned to the shoveling role, who have only used trowels on smaller mounds of dirt because in their previous roles they managed projects using forks and hoes in their end-to-end business processes—using the mentality that dirt is dirt, isn't it?

I don't know how many times I've had to teach my peers how to shovel, warned execs how many times they shouldn't take on large mounds of dirt without first estimating their mass (sizing a project), or picked up another person's mound because they are absolutely and completely useless at shoveling. With the managers who put them in the shoveling role, standing around going "Yes, how unfortunate, they clearly are the problem."

This, in a nutshell, is the problem.

People
Some final thoughts before getting into it.

I made a rather ugly and some would feel unfair claim earlier about people and I am pretty candid in this book. I know that claim can be summarized and interpreted a certain way as "I think most people in IT are bad at their jobs and therefore bad people." Or to summarize even further—"you suck!" Which even I admit is immature and was also the working title for the first four or five versions of this book; and that the claim denotes a complete value judgment on people which for the record I don't intend.

So just thought I'd say that no matter how horrible some of the people I have worked with seem to have been to others, no matter how clueless in their jobs they seem to have been, or how badly they've effected other people, I haven't met a single person I could not happily sit down with, outside of the work context, over a drink or a meal, and have a good chat.

This may seem a little hypocritical, but it's not, to quote some psychotherapeutic premise, I can't remember where it comes from: apparently we don't disapprove of the person, just the person's behavior.

Also in reentering the profession, and in terms of my agreements with PMI that enable me to maintain my PMP, I was just so overwhelmed by the atrocious level of project managing and caught up in the chaos that I forgot about a principal premise of PMI philosophy—if someone is in a job they are struggling with, the first thing to do (line-management aside) is to coach and educate.

I find it hard to do this while actively engaged within my profession, the tsunami of noise and stress—and sheer amount of poor practice causing them—prevent it, but I can sit down and quietly write a book about it.

I. PROJECT MANAGEMENT IN IT

We get some rules to follow
That and this
These and those
No one knows
Queens of the Stone Age: No One Knows

This section describes the most common poor practices occurring in project management today—from how projects are selected for implementation to how we incorrectly set them up, implement, and end them. I provide a description of poor practices around contract management, requirements management, governance, and day-to-day activities such as project, reporting, and change processes. I provide a commentary regarding incorrectly adopting standards and the affect of poorly performing human resources. The chapter concludes by breaking down poor practices that occur at the end of IT projects.

If you hired me, you would be disappointed if I gave you the paragraph synopsis from the introduction to explain your IT project management woes and rightly so—especially if I didn't give you the answers to fixing the problem. In the first versions of this book, I used very big words to summarize the fundamental issues I saw in IT and IT project management. It was like a complete, lessons-learned review. I've included it in the following list.

If I were to apply a project analysis regarding all organisations and projects I've dealt with in the last fifteen years—whether for a customer, a vendor, or as an advisor to either—my report would have the following findings:

- Cross-arm conflicts between business groups and IT or between business groups preventing alignment of IT objectives to business objectives
- Project selection and initiation processes clouded, immature, and projects without clear and measurable business objectives or business requirements
- No evidence of project forecasting, integrated planning, or tracking to any sort of baseline (baseline methodology) with project managers not displaying knowledge or experience in these areas—despite holding project management certifications
- Project managers unable to schedule or determine dependencies or understand the relevance or importance of these tasks
- Project managers, constrained by process, management, and/or lack of skill or experience who are little more than project leads or project administrators (as per the PMI definition) focusing only on day-to-day tasks outside of the context of a project process or activity and PRINCE2 definition of day-to-day management
- Basic project documentation not in evidence (as indicative of artifacts produced by good project process and controls)
- Project methodologies and frameworks utilized or put in place but not understood, followed, adhered to, or supported by senior management (exposed to: PRINCE2, PMBOK® GUIDE, SCRUM) with confusion regarding how to implement these toolsets and the differences between them

- Subject matter expertise and a good grasp of technical concepts seem to be required by project managers to successfully complete most IT projects and avoid their pitfalls (in contrary to some popular accepted views and theory) though not in evidence
- Role confusion across the project and technical space, including governance
- Immature acknowledgement of project management as a professional practice/core corporate/IT competency
- PMOs (project management offices) not understanding their purpose or the responsibilities that coincide with this corporate role
- Significant influx of resource from the business into IT positions with no understanding of what these positions involve nor basic IT principles
- Significant influx of resource into project related positions with no understanding of what these positions involve nor basic portfolio, programme, and project management principles

Wow those words sound great and look really impressive. But if we boil all these things down to the common denominator, what we come up with is that paragraph from the introduction. People are making mistakes that cause the patterns outlined above, which causes projects to fail. They are doing this because they don't have experience in *professional* project management. When I say professional project management I mean the application of proven and successful practices from our global project management bodies. Perhaps the problem is a result of the lack of a country that treats project management as a real profession like law or medicine.

Also in terms of remedying the situation described by my very big words, there's no use following standard project management book writing to remedy this situation; i.e., that I list the tools and processes, their reasoning and importance, and finally give step-by-step examples of how to walk through those original issues listed.

What would be the point?

There are thousands of books and courses that attempt to remedy the situation in this way. Half of us who call ourselves IT PMs and have already read those types of books or attended those types of courses and received qualifications. But nothing is changing. Doing the same, prescriptive thing is not going to improve things and hasn't to date. Or as I like to put it;

The definition of insanity is listening to Hotel California over and over again, and expecting a different result.[1]

Yet I do feel the need to conform to the status quo and provide a book on my take on how to complete basic project tasks and why we should do them. My peers would be proud. There'd be pats on my back in a kind of technocratic, self-congratulatory manner that meant we all knew this was happening and it was good that I'd produced the same solution that hasn't fixed any problems so far. They would say *thanks for not actually rocking the boat because none of us really want to face the reality—that we do actually suck at this*!

You see in the first versions of this book I wanted to make dramatic claims like "Whatever it is we're doing it's not project management!" and "We say we're project managers, but we aren't!," but what I've experienced is so prolific, so widespread and ingrained in how IT projects are run that it's got me thinking. If something is so endemic that it's considered by everyone as standard practice, when people like me turn around and use standard project management practice to point out the actual basics—either to an audience of glazed looks or one where I am viewed as some sort of magician conjuring up future impact assessments from dependency mappings—the common poor practice really *is* standard practice even if it's poor. The

---

1 Great song, best lead break (in the context of the song it is in) ever! Currently on repeat.)

methodology books are wrong. The theories are good in theory but aren't standing up in practice.

We better cover what project management in IT actually is.

Project Selection: The Real Reasons for doing Projects

I'm sure the projects you're involved with in IT are sold to you as pieces of some great, overarching, integrated plan. They're strategically aligned, based on the needs of an ever-growing and ever-changing business, well thought out, and provided with a clear set of achievable business objectives (yes business objectives, not technical objectives) —which themselves have been translated into clear, concise requirements.

Or not...

To recap the theoretical project selection process (known as Starting up a Project in PRINCE2) is where embryonic projects—some little more than ideas—are assessed against the need of the business, the direction of IT and the business it serves, and even against other potential projects to gauge the project's merits. Here is supposed to be the start for business case development.

However, if this process happens at all, for the majority of organisations and their IT initiatives, the process is normally missing key activities and rigor around business justification. Related strategic alignments are little more than alchemy with most people involved in the process not really knowledgable of the broader business and technical elements as an integrated and related whole. Nor are they aware how IT initiatives should be translated and defined into something that can be justified and that justification measured.

In my experience, here are the top eleven "business reasons" IT projects start—with the business case and justification a posthumous afterthought.

1. A manager plucked it out of the air – so just do it (run the project).
2. A manager says "I have no understanding of what we're doing or why senior management want it, but I don't want to get fired so you have to run this project."
3. It's the latest trend in technology. Everyone in our industry is implementing it and I don't want to look like an idiot when I have drinks with my exec/CIO peers. By the way if you stuff it up, you're fired.
4. I have a budget I need to spend.
5. It's our latest product—your company needs it.
6. The associated product launch has already been announced publically and you have to meet the public launch date—regardless of the actual size and complexity of the associated project.
7. The project was being run as Business As Usual (BAU) by another business arm and has been handed to your PMO.
8. It's about enterprise architecture—provided by a misinformed and inexperienced enterprise architect (EA) who less than four years ago was a marketing manager and has only ever read a book on Enterprise Architecture, was really good at managing servers for a specific environment in a previous role, or has actually specified an implementation plan using methods that are ten years out of date.
9. It's part of our IT strategy—old, poorly defined, and never anchored in the needs of the business.
10. A CIO says "Platform ABC implementation is part of our three to five year plan so we have to do it."—based on a plan not fully completed or integrated with an IT or business strategy let alone a consolidated programme of work.

11. A senior Systems Administrator has told senior management that "We have to upgrade System ABC because we bought this piece of junk software with crap functionality that met only half the requirements after it was implemented (not that we know what requirements are or have ever defined them—it just doesn't work properly), and the glue and string we've built around it in the meantime won't work otherwise."

These are the reasons IT projects are born to fail. IT projects fail and project management goes awry when we can't hold business justification to the flame and assess the business need and hence can't judge if implementation or development was successful.

Its worse when people decide to protect their roles at nearly any cost, and when people suppress any real attempt at defining the business objectives (let's face it, this will bite them in the arse when the real cost of the project is known). Think about it. If we were visibly and ultimately responsible for an IT project that was based on real business need and had clear objectives all involved understood and agreed on, we would not promote an operations team business manager to IT PM because they're related on our wife or husband's side, or they want to be a project manager, or they have the word "manager" in their title so might as well halo them into the PM role. But we *would* make sure we had the best experienced PM available and surround them and the project with the most mature, robust PM practices and people possible

Really, terminally, that's it. It's the end of any chance of a project being successful. No project can succeed when they are selected using any of the eleven reasons to start a project listed above as a "project selection process" —with vague or non-eistent selection criteria. With inexperienced people running the selection processes, there's no way any IT project can be measured for success during its implementation with vague or nonexistent selection criteria.

Even if there is a project selection process that resembles the theo-retical one, there is rarely a good understanding of IT and IT projects and their relationship to the business. How can there be when the IT operations manager was, up until a few years ago, an operations manager for a tuna fish production factory and has no real expere-ince with or knowledge of basic IT principles, or the current CIO has been promoted into their position via the Peter Principle? How can there be when the business executive manager now responsi-ble to the CEO for their IT portfolio has no background in IT? This person never really understood all this IT stuff, didn't rate anyone in IT because of the reasons in this book, and doesn't have any experi-ence in project management.

These inexperienced people can have no idea how much IT pro-jects and systems really cost–not just because no one has been able to accurately estimate those costs for them during a man-aged project selection process, but because they are inexperi-enced; IT is too expensive, so these projects are going to pay for it somehow.

Project Management as a core competency? Yes, for senior manage-ment and executives, that means we actually have to learn some-thing new. At the turn of the century IT was just starting to be iden-tified as a core corporate competency for competitive advantage or real efficiency gains (Our IT systems need to be providing efficiency gains in our business or providing us with an advantage against our competitors. We don't just have IT systems because that's the way it is.). It wasn't that long ago. Has anyone assessed in their selection processes what happens when two tightly coupled and immature supporting areas such as project management and information technology are applied (collide) in business? Well try picturing those zombie film sequences where everyone is running about screaming, trying to fight the zombies, gradually getting mauled and turned. This is what happens when these two immature supporting areas collide in business.

Cynically perhaps, it should be the end of the book. It's because of these immature or nonexistent selection processes that IT projects fail, but a) the book's not long enough to be published yet and b) we carry on with these projects despite the shortcomings in our selection processes.

Project Initiation: How we Stuff it up from the Start

◇◇

Ok now we're doing the wrong projects for wrong or nonexistent reasons.

And guess what? We're already late. This is because the programme, PMO, project delivery, account, business, or area managers who have no real understanding of project initiation (read: have never actually managed a project!) were accountable for getting a project to this stage and were in charge of early planning and communications. This has already caused the project to be over budget, under scoped, under resourced, and late. So very, very late. These people don't have the experience to know the delivery date should be changed accordingly or have been just plain vindictive and wanted to pressure all involved in getting the project running by being obtuse (this is very common in IT).

Pity the poor fool that takes this one on...oh wait...that's me and my fellow PMs! As we enter the valley, first it's finding and contracting the right vendors for the work.

Contracts

Two words: "fair" and "reasonable." That's it. A contract should be fair and reasonable to all parties. It should pinch all parties a little bit so there's everyone has a stake in the game. A contract needs to be constructed or worded so that all parties can be successful at the end of their work; it should be, ideally, constructed together, collaboratively—it should not be an adversarial process.

So why are customers holding the "fixed price" like an axe over the head's of vendors like some demented, masked axe man of doom? Why are vendors hiding behind the padding of the "fixed price" blanket, chortling away to themselves as their customers' projects blow out with extras that should have been at the very least controlled against an original baseline?[2] If a vendor is more astute than customers, then customers we're in for a world of hurt as we take on padding that is burning our budgets. Likewise, vendors, if we're at all constrained by service agreements, unreasonable customer expectations, unclear requirements, or vague breakout clauses for managing change and defining success, then we might as well give up as we'll never break-even—let alone keep profit margins. While we're at it, let's get competing vendors trying to work alongside each other but ensure we don't have management clauses for interaction so we can giggle mercilessly as we watch them struggle and scream and claw their way through our project—cock fight anyone?

So here we are, past selection, late into initiation, and now we have the arguments, process constraints, sign offs, and general battle to maintain whatever scope has been defined and translate it into something someone, somewhere, can actually do. But it seems that it takes time and money to define the work further—uh oh! No one's accounted for this! Now we're even more over budget or already eating into whatever risk margin both parties have accepted; more commonly at the very worst, let's leave the work poorly defined and under scoped, fix the price, and see how we go. Let's make those cocky vendors pay for the audacity to actually ask for money for this phase—it should be free shouldn't and they should know this stuff already. What is all this project management and requirements stuff anyway?

Let's get them on the back foot and keep them there under the passive aggressive auspice of a "partnership"—this is where we blame them for

---

2 For the answers to the rhetorical "why" in this paragraph read the rest of this book.

the last five years of our IT mistakes. And because we're so time and dollar poor, let's use the contract as a project management plan! Why not? After all it's got a work breakdown structure (kind of) and some guidance at what needs to be done. What else could we need?

Requirements

Normally we've already started by the time some poor sap in a tiny little voice asks for requirements. You know—those things that map the objectives into slices and parcels of needs and wants so that we can figure out if and when we've done something successfully. Then build a solution that meets those needs and wants—whether we've adopted a product focus or not.

But that would be far too easy. Instead, let's have weeks and endless rounds of discussions, teleconferences, idea sessions, side stepping and argumentative finger pointing as we try to define the work without using the tools of definition and avoid the massive holes developing in the contract at the same time! To make it better, let's get this happening while we're dealing with the contracts and get the guys started in building the solution now to keep on time. What could possibly go wrong with this approach? How hard can it be? An e-mail system is an e-mail system; a financial system is a financial system! Why can't we just get it in and go have a beer?

It was too quiet anyway. We need this noise to seem busy, get stressed, and disguise the fact that—mostly—no one knows what the hell they're doing, why they're doing it, when they need to get it done by, and how much effort should be spent doing it. If only we had some way of organizing decision making, ownership, authority, and above all else accountability and structure to manage rapid and significant change.

Governance

Now we're at the initiation stage with all sorts of shrapnel whizzing around our heads (remember the grenade went off during project selection). Didn't someone mention we should have something called governance for every project? You know that thing whereby our egos are inflated by giving us fantastic titles in yet another hierarchy. Where we get to show up to yet more meetings (shows we're busy!) and yell at those odd characters called project managers.

I mean we already have responsibilities in our day job, so this must be some special form of reward to attend boards, working groups, and associated project meetings while just sitting there doing nothing but looking good and feeling important. If we're lucky we may even get that title of project executive—bonus!

Or even better let's not do it. It seems too hard and we just don't understand why it would be needed. There seems to be enough happening already without us adding to the situation and time is money!

No, no, I know! We'll grab a project human resource hierarchy from somewhere else. Without seeing if it suits this project, we'll assign people to it who have no skin in the game, and then as everyone starts whining because this is the latest thing and they haven't been invited to join in (got to keep people happy) we'll keep inviting people in the governance positions until, until, until...we have a committee! Yes! Now we're cooking! The more the merrier! This will make any decision making fast, efficient, and practical. What did you say? It'll help cover our arses and spread the blame when something goes terribly and tragically wrong. But no, surely not. Projects work this way!

So don't fret. There's enough of us involved now to make sure this thing can't go wrong!

We Haven't Even Started Yet!

So it's here where IT projects fail...erm...I think I said that already... OK. It's also here that IT projects fail...ah, no that won't work either because they've already failed at the selection phase. This is a tough one. OK, if they've failed at the selection phase then its here where projects nose dive into a downward spiral of chaos that can't really be recovered from...ah, much better.

Project Implementation: Making Bad Things Worse

ow we're doing the wrong projects for no real reason without
structure in place for control and without actually knowing what
we're doing.

Ah, chaos! Thou sound so sweet.

The Day-To-Day of it

Now that we're through selection and initiation, as project managers what is it we do day-to-day in the face of the overwhelming amount of noise and chaos presented to us when we adopt a new project for execution—the tumultuous rapids of insanity that is IT project management implementation? Do we make an effort to wrangle the present into the shape of the future and vice versa?

No, we do day-to-day stuff. We focus on the now. We only focus on the current major issue or next technical change that needs to be completed—and the next person screaming on the phone at us. On both sides, vendor and customer, we sit there and treat our job and the projects we are working on as if they are some ongoing service provision with endless tomorrows and unending buckets of budget. Just to make it easier to get things done, don't forget the unending, incorrectly implemented mass of Information Techonolgy Infrastructure Library (ITIL) processes we jump through hoops for to get the simplest thing completed.

We don't keep planning. We don't keep forecasting or tracking either. We don't even check the scope or the contract we are working let alone translate it into something everyone can understand (that would be something).

As customer project managers we wonder why the software build is always late, why the infrastructure won't talk across logical network boundaries, and we laugh—how we laugh—at those vendor project managers who can't seem to get their act together. Haha! It's OK; we'll get them at the next project meeting and embarrass them in front of others by accusing them of things they can't possibly argue against without spending massive amounts of time trolling through the endless e-mail trails we use for documentation and decision tracking. Or because the vendor project managers can never get their act together, at end of month cycle when we won't pay them— haha, how we'll laugh then.

We sit there day after day figuring out how we can cover ourselves, our management, and our company. That's what we do. Knowing that and seeing things going wrong, we apply massive amounts of effort reacting, managing, and structuring things so that we don't get shown up and projects look like they're on track; finger-pointing when we can't make the projects look healthy.

We try desperately to get things done in the coming week or two (maximum), stumbling our way through the maelstrom around us like a ship without a rudder caught in a massive storm.

We swap out PMs and technical staff because we haven't planned resource properly and are now too stretched to complete anything. Then the replacements jump like idiots on fire as they pick up the mess and try to get things done on time and understand what it is we're doing. However, they never quite catch up, never quite understand the shape of the project that was handed to them. Then as PMs we wonder why budgets are 200 to 400 percent over and why the technical staff has burned hundreds of additional hours completing extra work.

Then we turn around and blame the last PM, engineer, or consultant for the mess that's occurring. At least this gives our management something to talk about at their next meeting, and then no one left around has to be held accountable. Perfect. Well done, guys.

As customers we sit there and day after day hold vendors completely accountable for our cock-ups, for our lack of understanding of our business, for project management in general, and for the technical landscape we work in. We get into the blame shifting game, spend hours tripping over ourselves while we try and figure out what is going wrong, why vendors aren't communicating with each other, and spend endless amounts of time trying to come up with creative reasons why we need more budget and time. And then (oh the irony is rich), if the project is important enough, we turn around and hire someone like me!

We come in at a premium rate, review projects, and try to get them back on track. But we can't make the lost money magically come back. By the time we get to it most of the budget has been sunk on meaningless, ineffectual rubbish. And if we dare mention sunk cost, there are heart attacks because they're pretty much the only two words that will float above our levels by themselves and reach the board whether we want them to or not.

As vendors, we are so afraid of losing the client because of the managed service contract or software licensing our company provides. We can't tell the client what is actually wrong on their side or ours, and so become even more ineffectual as we are constrained in our ability to maneuver the project to avoid company and customer risk (and actually deliver anything to the customer) for fear of treading on others feet and the account itself. When we need it the most, we can't afford the premium help because roles like that don't directly turn a profit, and our PMO and management to the board level isn't mature enough to accept that "fix it" (practice) roles must be hired in (when things have gone wrong), and that they are actually indirectly and inversely profitable.

To conclude, we're basically vague, obtuse, and rude to our peers. We have no idea what project management is. Let's face it, up until a few years ago most of us were in another industry, area of IT, or business arm and decided to complete PRINCE2. We have completed no other project management training and have no idea how to forecast or complete other basic project management tasks because PRINCE2 does not focus on project management techniques!

We set unrealistic timeframes because we can't get our act together to plan our own parts. We act like toddlers and throw tantrums in the worst way. Once the noise of previous phase problems reach that crescendo pitch of complete and utter chaos, we simply hand it all on to someone else, get a different project to manage, or management steps in and smoothes it all over. The financial loss is accepted or massaged into another area or financial period. The scapegoat and their boss gets a severe telling off. Those responsible—namely the ones that aren't there and can't answer for themselves—are forever noted for the cock up. You better believe it, but don't fear it, as it has to be mind-numbingly bad before anyone remaining on project is ever held accountable for it and then fired.

Process is as Process Does—Or Not

To specify this, there is a huge difference between accepted project processes and processes that seem to fill up an IT PM's day.

These are not defined project processes:

- Attending a meeting (such as change control)
- Calling a vendor/customer

- Writing a statement of work
- Calling a vendor/customer again
- E-mailing someone
- Tracking a package/delivery and making sure it arrives
- Following up
- E-mailing someone else
- Creating a spreadsheet
- Making sure an engineer or developer completes work
- Browsing the Internet for the latest sports results or shopping
- Filling out our weekly report
- Approving resource time
- Arranging technical changes to occur
- Talking to our boss about finances

The list goes on, but none of these things are, in themselves, project processes, but this is what is commonly accepted as project management for IT. In other words, IT project management seems to involve the following: do this thing, call it a project, and chuck mud at it till it sticks by *doing things that any other office worker would do in their day-to-day activities, but without understanding accepted and proven project management techniques.*

As IT PMs, our actions rarely result in a commonly accepted process or activity output according to the PMBOK ® Guide or PRINCE2 definitions. We are not really completing project management—at best we are completing some directionless administrative task and at worse we are completing a meaningless action contributing to our constant position behind the eight ball.

This is *not* project management! This is why a "programme manager" once stood before me and the person we were working for and said, "I don't see the point of [project] forecasting" as we were trying to establish a basic project tracker with the person. How could they make such a *insertwordhere* statement, demonstrating a complete lack of understanding around process, programme, and project management themes? Some of the most caustic problems I see in IT project management are caused by project managers who are not aware of or don't implement project management processes and activities.

We only focus on the "do"—the day-to-day office activities. We fail to understand the application of what we're qualified to do.

To boil it down, because ITPMs

- Are only doing the day-to-day office activities like the ones listed above and not practicing the processes and activities that structure a project (like are described in the PMBOK® Guide and PRINCE2) in the context of their parts/phases/ stages/whatever
- Aren't completing at least one of the four actions from the PDCA cycle every single hour of every single day of project management in IT (see PDCA section later on in this book)

IT project management—if it can be called that—is failing.

Most IT PMs can't see past the wall of noise in front of them. They don't have a tool to get through the noise or any idea where they are in a project month-to-month, week-to-week, day-to-day, and in some cases hour-to-hour. Our project managers are ships without compasses and rudders in a seething sea of storms and violent winds— and we hired them. They wonder why they are constantly on the back foot? Here's some inside information from someone who has worked as a vendor, as a customer, and as a consultant: on any given project we're involved with, most if not all of the PMs involved are like this whether they're a vendor or a customer. All of them are on the back foot, so we should stop laughing at them and pointing fingers when things go wrong. Most ITPMs are all in the same boat—because of the issues covered in this book—not because they are all bad at their jobs.

Worse, we set our PMOs up with processes that have little if anything to do with defined project management processes and activities. We focus on getting the monthly finance process sorted, the
reports process done. We spend inordinate amounts of time developing PMO methodologies with processes that remain the management and progression of our project contracts we've mistaken for
total project management.[3]

It comes down to this: If a PM can't describe (and their delivery or
PMO manager cannot explain) what defined project processes or
activities should be occuring (not pointless PMO processes or day-
to-day activities), how to do them, why they should be doing them,
and where a project is today and how it's getting to where it should
be next week, project management is not happening.

I know what will help! Let's get some reporting happening so we can
closely analyze what our projects are doing, that'll save us!

Pretty Colours
Green, amber, and red.

Complete chaos is occurring and what do we do? Create coloured
dashboards so that we look like we're in control to our sponsors or
management.

Yet somehow we're aware they know that the processes that went
in to building these "tools" are arbitrary because they are based on
something that will not stand up to close scrutiny or analysis. They
know that the processes themselves change month to month, creating not just a moving goalpost but an entire moving stadium because
the people creating the dashboards are making it up as they go
along. Ultimately, even the most clueless of us know that the pretty
coloured sheet in front of us is worthless.

---

3 Yes I know, something is better than nothing—more on that later

And OK so we all know what green means—happy happy days. But what does amber mean? What does red mean? What do I need to do if I see these colours? What are you doing if these colours are present, and what does it mean for the project? What if a project is all green and yet you're asking me for more budget, time, or resource? Should I be worried?

In eighteen years of IT and IT project management I've only seen two dashboards that represented a great deal of the truth and that could be used even at the board level for problem assessment and decision making. Two!

"But we used the project reports to build the dashboard" I hear you plead.

Yeah. About that. You mean we used the status reports that are produced irregularly, get massaged beyond recognition in most reporting periods to give the right answer, and are politically correct or outright censored as a basis for the dashboard—which has meaningless headings because few of us actually know what tracking against a forecast or baseline actually means.

I've completed hours of forensics against all sorts of IT projects from software development to massive infrastructure changes, accessing financial systems, project reports, and tracking systems (that is, if tracking systems exist). Unquestionably I find that none of these things relate! It's as if under the guise of project managers, our project managers have done anything but project management!

There's not an auditable trail of project management mistakes when a project is reviewed because there is no trail of project management. Just a seemingly random series of events and bad decisions tied together by a company identifier, code, or name that ends in the word "project."

And I find that we are using these reporting tools incorrectly as a process rather than the result of one (or several). We are so busy paying lip service to their purpose and ultimately developing our own project empire (or covering our arse, or both) that by the time someone responsible for the budget and its outputs sees them, they are in fact fiction.

No matter! At least while the maelstrom of day-to-day "management" is happening and reports are being generated, we're still focused on the right thing.

Change is Change is Change

What is it that adds to the noise? What is it we spend the majority of the time actually doing in IT project management? That thing that always makes us feel always a few steps behind events, always firefighting, and always explaining to our management or the customer why it's screwed up yet again.

No, PMI, it's not communication. Not really.

It's change.

We manage change. We manage complex change. We manage rapid, complex change across all levels of a project. We manage rapid complex change, across all levels of a project, occurring at the same time. No, that's not quite right. Sorry. I meant to say we fail to manage rapid, complex change that happens across all levels of a project, occurring at the same time.

To be fair, there's a lot of change in IT projects. More so—I have gathered from feedback by project managers outside IT—per scope per project. There are two things I want to say about the amount of change in IT projects.

The first is that there shouldn't be that much change, not at the fundamental levels of a project. If the early project processes were completed even remotely correctly, a great deal of change would be settled before we got to execution. But alas, it's even noisier, with change considered, that we never nail what it is we're doing. Because of this, we quickly become change's bitches. You know that feeling we get when we've just nailed something down, and another piece of the puzzle flares up just out of reach. The puzzle needs to be defined thoroughly first!

The second thing I want to say about how poorly we manage change is that it's because we misunderstand it. We don't identify its levels or impact it has at each level. Because of this, our project managers and technical staff are only focusing on the next technical implementations, which unfortunately are called "changes"— thanks, ITIL!

When cleaning up the projects we, our project managers, and our vendor's or customer's project managers have made a mess of, I find (at least for infrastructure projects) that the only "change" we've been managing are technical changes (change management). For development projects the only "change" we've been managing is functional interpretations and discrepancies—and retrospectively at that.

These are both such narrow definitions of change within any IT project. Both are onerous and time consuming processes. This is because ITIL is a little vague when it comes to telling us how to do "change management" and hardly mention projects at all (twice in the version currently in use at the time of writing). Also, no one has bothered to set SMART requirements. So much so that we forget to, or just don't, manage any other form of change.

Scope changes are vaguely managed by asking a vendor to create a contract variation—that's all we need to do, really? Resource changes are not managed, and a lip service handover is all that happens because we haven't allowed budget for proper handovers to be completed. (That's right! If there are two PMs or engineers conducting a handover, that's twice the effort and most likely twice the cost.)

Environmental changes in the technical space occur rapidly and regularly, yet no one manages these in terms of programme interaction and BAU activity. The impacts this level of change will have on fundamental things such as technical approaches to completing project activities and project timelines are significant. It's even worse when there are multiple vendors looking after our environments and we have to deal with multiple (incomplete) BAU and programme schedules (if there are any).

So what do we do? We get angry. We get mad. We start finger pointing and whining. We stand there like rabbits in the glare from the headlights of a car when Mr. Significant Change comes along and kicks us in the genitals time after time after time.

We just aren't looking for it let alone ready for it. We're so surprised that this happens. That budgets double and PMs spend inordinate amounts of time in "change management" that they get nothing else done. That the business changes their minds and that some of us involved are generally so clueless about our jobs that we forget to table some crucial piece of information that will change a crucial aspect of the project.

What could possibly save us?

Going Around in Circles
A project methodology.

Someone has come along and wants us to adopt the SCRUM process framework for developing complex products throughout the PMO—to use for all our projects, including infrastructure projects.

Someone has misread a government project management review. The recommendation to use the PRINCE2 project management methodology (geared for simple projects) to ensure better chance of project success, has now been interpreted as a decree that PRINCE2 should be used for all government IT projects, no matter how complex they are.

Agile. Now that sounds like an answer to all our problems! Let's do that. Let's run all phases and stages of projects using agile, whether they need it or not. What's agile again?

No forget Agile. PMI and PMBOK, that's the methodology for us...er, that's not a methodology!

Didn't someone tell us never to use the waterfall method? What? Why not? What if it's perfect for a project? "Oh no, no one uses waterfall anymore. There are studies saying we shouldn't" you tell me. Correction: there are studies saying we shouldn't blindly apply it across all IT projects, especially large developmental projects!

Very few of us seem to understand what PRINCE2, SCRUM, the PMBOK® Guide, actually are, how to implement them, what they mean, and their pitfalls. Most of us wouldn't know the difference between a methodology, framework, and toolset if they all came up and whacked us in the head. Again, the thought has crossed my mind frequently.

Really, these grouping of common project management resources do have one thing in common, and it's the thing that I find so very few of us have acknowledged. That is, these resources all caution and warn about first assessing what methodology or framework is right for our organisation *before* implementing them, never recommending wholesale implementations or implementation without tailoring.

But unfortunately, many of the people we hire into PMO management or project delivery management roles have never actually run a project before, let alone created a platform for running projects.

An even littler known fact is that these methodologies, frameworks, and project approaches *are not mutually exclusive*! Any IT PMO should have a mixture of each because each *manages project risk and delivery in a slightly different way*. I cover this in later sections.

Unfortunately, we continue to let those with little or no background in project management instruct our PMOs without guidance. Then we expect our project managers, already dealing with an absolute nightmare described above, to actually do anything remotely productive.

Why are we surprised at the project overruns and derailments we are experiencing? We haven't been doing the rounds with the board and exec team about project management as a core corporate competency. So why should we expect that our processes, if based in project management methodologies and frameworks at all, would be tailored to the needs of our organisations and their projects. More importantly, how do we know these processes are fit for purpose?

But at least we've got the right people on the job.

Cowboys, Plumbers, Fiddlers, and Jokers

I want to be careful here and acknowledge that there is a great deal of good people in and around this profession, and I take my hat off to them...

...and provide hats to the others...

First up is the cowboy hat; this goes to those technical resources—and project managers—who fire from the hip, make changes without telling anyone, don't have the experience they said they had at the recruitment interview, and basically go through life with (metaphorically though sometimes literally) slicked back hair and a "devil may care" attitude. They screw up systems and projects left, right, and centre. The kind of resource where we have to go behind them and mend whatever it was they broke. They have such a problem with authority that they are basically unusable on a project—as if projects weren't hard enough!

Next up are the plumbers; these humble and micro-task-orientated technical resources who stumble along until they come to a problem, stop, and don't tell anyone. Awesome! What's that I hear you say? It's not your problem? How can it be anyone else's problem but yours if you aren't communicating? What? You didn't have to put up with this kind of thing when you were in BAU? Well OK, back to BAU you go! Please note: BAU and service delivery resources are *not* project resources; they will drain our projects of budget by adding time—so much time. Unless trained and supported in the nature and application of projects, BAU technical resources will not adhere to any concept of time bound delivery, and will probably be working on something else when we expect them to be working on our project! Priority One operational issues (P1s) are P1s after all—and obviously more important than that multi-million dollar IT project spiralling out of control.

Then there are those cuddly fiddlers with no concept of responsibility to the business, unable to realize that at the end of production systems there is a real business running, with no respect for project and technical work authority or any agreed scope. These people are just plain dangerous to have around, and will add many hours of effort as we try to regain trust with our customer/business arm. In the end, someone else cleans up after them.

Lastly, there are the jokers—that's us, the project managers. We're a joke. Most technical roles and some management in IT think we're a joke, especially if we're not technical, and especially if we've been haloed into the role and don't really know what it's about. Couple that with the screaming chaos that we've been hired to manage and don't—or can't even. It's no wonder we're often the laughingstock of our IT peers.

All these types of resources are killing our project execution, but we are so resource poor and unaware of what is required from technical resources in IT (let alone IT projects) that we hire them anyway...

...ah man is the project over yet?

Project Closure: This is The End, Beautiful Friend...

◇◇◇

N o, it's not. Most IT projects never end.

Software development projects never end because scope is conveniently truncated into "new releases"—because the delivery scope that had been drawn up was incorrectly sized and not managed during execution, producing significantly less features for the buck. So now we have to run another project (or more likely keep the current project going) to deliver what we originally set out to deliver. In addition, we're still using waterfall to run software projects and waiting until the very end of these projects before checking that the software is working as was originally intended.

In this situation everyone's so happy with the new arrangement—to (utterly) rescope now that the proverbial is about to hit the fan—and to have missed this close call, that no one tracks back to the cause of the problem. No one reviews the sizing tools, estimation techniques, and benefits the work was meant to produce.

Business customers don't really understand what has happened or why they've received half the functions they thought they were getting. But IT management agrees a first point release and a couple of "free upgrades" because they've invested too much in the developer vendor—including sickly coupling their own processes with the developer's, so that the developer almost becomes part of the family.

The developer, whether they want it or not, now has huge power over the customer and—don't forget—is also trying to cover themselves before their execs find out what's really happened.

In other instances of software projects that never end, ongoing and unchecked rounds of "what did we miss?' in the guise of ongoing requirements gathering gets smeared over poorly managed development iterations by people who don't know how to define requirements.

In these situations developers are too busy struggling with the ongoing problems in the development environment. This happens primarily because no one came up with a clear set of nonfunctional requirements. The environment has to keep changing to keep up with the new influx of functional requirements and external (to the project) environmental influences. Technical debt is difficult to manage because very few know what this is and fewer make allowances for the additional effort and budget in their projects or in their sales model.

Infrastructure projects also never end and go on, and on, and on.

This is because no one is managing programme influences and technical resources are scarce and are constantly shifted between projects, so work is never finished. More prevalently, the project has churned through project managers on all sides, so by the time a halfway decent project manager gets placed on the project, no one can remember exactly what the project was doing in the first place. All this occurs until the original reason for the scope becomes redundant and/or is superseded with a more advanced programme or even technology in some cases.

Then a project dies without reviewing what went wrong. Don't even ask about reviewing what went right. Please! Lessons learnt and project reviews, if completed, seem little more than self-aggrandizements. We congratulate ourselves for getting (the wrong) stuff done (badly), and breathe a collective sigh of relief that it's over. The issues that have caused the original eight-week programme to last for fifteen months and cost three times as much as anyone had envisaged are swept under the carpet.

Other projects never end because a PM or business owner just continually adds to the list of things to do until a project becomes "ongoing." Additions to the original scope never go through a selection and initiation process, and investment is never assessed. All this happens because, primarily, the original solution was ill-conceived, had no business requirements placed against it, and was attempted with no structured approach to design and testing.

By the time we ask for people in project recovery to reign in these monsters, their momentum is considerable and so ingrained into programme that we resist the obvious: to kill the project in its tracks and hold those responsible accountable for the train crash and prevent them from ever running something like this again until significant help and coaching is provided. We should always reassess the investment, purpose, and benefit of continuing any project. But by the end everyone has their "run and hide" hats on, shifting the blame where possible, becoming vague and forgetful, and generally behaving badly. The last man standing is the person who has the longest and most complete e-mail trail.

The best example of this is the PM that I replaced on a 400 percent budget overrun and eighteen month runaway who—get this—removed any record of the project and its decisions from the files for the companies he was working with and then fled the country! What's more, I saw the PM just the other day, back in the country about twelve months after the individual had left, talking to a PM recruitment agent over coffee.

What are people in recovery roles left with— the people brought in to an organisation to fix these abominations? Don't forget that we recovery folks like the people we work for, no matter what's going down or how frustrated we get. Now we have the task of giving the people in these organisations—left holding on to these project nightmares—the bad news.

This type of bad news always equates to a smoking crater so big that it damages the organisation's budgets and profit to the point of negating further investment for vast tracks of its entire portfolio! It damages the organisation's reputation and relationships with vendors and customers. Us recovery folks then have to explain that while the PM on the project origionally really was a villain, he or she could only get away with it because the monitoring and controlling processes in the PMO the organisation had in place, were so immature that we could have hid an entire portfolio of these projects in the gaps and holes we also found in their PMO processes; that ultimately it's the responsibility of the person that put the PM in that role in the first place. That reasoning goes up the management chain until someone who knows their job well is found. You see that in management (theory at least) it's their mistake, not the mistakes of the staff and contractors underneath them.

The bright side is that this can be fixed, but the truly demoralising aspect is that no matter how much all of us nod and implement the process change that will "fix the issues," within a year or two we (or our replacements) are dealing with the same issues.

As to whether we kill these projects or not, the cost of figuring out what's going on adds to the original budget, and there is considerable effort involved in recovering these behemoths.

It is sometimes incredibly hard to track just what has gone wrong in terms of producing a trail that will withstand the scrutiny from the exec/board or a (subsequent) professional audit. It is harder still to assess and then dress the findings so that management won't blow their top when they read them, and then deflect their accountability by accusing the one producing them of being a doom and gloom merchant. And finally, it's hard to then try to maneuver the findings into the right place in the reporting hierarchy for resolution and action.

Another hardship is when the law has been trod on, overstepped, or completely broken.

Often times absolutely no one anywhere near the project and its associated line management has the faintest clue what is happening or how bad things really are.

Hardest yet is the fact that recovery people like me and their processes are disliked because they "show people up," and show people's bosses up. These roles "dob in" someone we like in the PMO because it's their made-up processes that primarily supported the issue and allowed some pseudo-PM to do the damage. Time after time we shoot the messenger.

Finally, inevitably, we kill a project. There's almost a palpable relief that passes amongst the techs on a project when it is euthanized or finally comes to a grinding halt. Like some irritation has finally had salve placed on it. There is the equivalent of a fresh summer breeze that flows gracefully over the associated management when the dust has settled and a project has been put to death. This lasts for but a fleeting moment, enough for everyone to sigh, or relax a little, and then...

...and then we start all over again.

2. CONTRIBUTING FACTORS

Is this the real life?
Is this just fantasy?
Caught in a landslide,
No escape from reality
Queen: Bohemian Rhapsody

This section overviews the wider influences affecting poor practices in IT project management, including treatments of the organisations and society in which we run projects. It ends with a brief self-assessment of my own history in project management to add context to the true extent of poor practice and subsequent chapters.

So far I've presented a pretty harsh synopsis of IT project management and sometimes emphasized it in a frustrated manner, but not by much. And yes, there are many areas in IT project management where things are getting better. But really, while my passion for my job has turned into frustration, it is still an accurate description of what I've experienced in IT project management. However, it doesn't stand alone; projects and IT don't occur in vacuums. These problems are occurring in a multilayered, multidimensional, and fantastic thing we call society, with all of its structures, organisations, systems, rules, regulations, and quirks.

Organisational Fun

Generals gathered in their masses
Just like witches at black masses
Evil minds that plot destruction
Sorcerer of death's construction
War Pigs: Black Sabbath

Wouldn't it be great to blame absolutely everything on bad management? I don't even need to define "bad management" further because it's so ingrained in our society that there are now even parodies of this phenomenon across popular culture (*Office Space*, *The Office*, and Dilbert comics come to mind).

We all know what it is. It's either that egotistic and seemingly bereft middle and upper management, completely detached from and plaguing the reality of the organisations they serve, haloed into their positions by either nepotism or the Peter Principle, or those villains closeted away like evil magicians, working malign machinations against the humble and innocent employee. But you know what? As much as we would love to heap the blame on these guys, we can't—not completely. Ultimately, while it's not always management's fault, it is always management's responsibility to deal with issues, but putting the blame squarely on management misses some crucial details.

For a start, the "conspiracy theories" just don't add up. If management is so intentionally terrible and ultimately against their employees, that means every other "bad management" theory must be inherently wrong. How can these guys be the agents of mass manipulation if they are as thick as two planks? How can they plan and implement such inconceivably nasty pestilences upon the unsuspecting if they can't manage their way out of a wet paper bag?

While it's convenient—and sometimes correct in particular and personal instances—to assign total culpability on someone else—in this case management, it sounds to me like another broad sweeping generalization that wouldn't stand up to much scrutiny. If I was to be flippant, then my money would be on the "bad (as in can't breathe and tap their fingers at the same time) management," but what does that make me, as I'm now part of management? There just seems to be far too many other things in play for any of these interpretations to hold true—things we all need to take a long, cold stare at.

Bad Management?

I was having lunch with a friend and colleague a while ago who is a really smart person, self-motivated, and works overseas for a large very specialized software and operations company. We began talking about Amazon publishing and this book, amongst other things, including coping techniques for "bad management" in projects, and she said the most amazing thing. She said, "I guess we should have a project manager on the project, and I guess I should say something, but really, if I said something, I'd have to actually do some work." I laughed with her.

She went on further to explain that the project was already fifteen months late; she'd told their management it would be late at least twelve months ago and that it had had a project manager but he'd been "pants," so management got rid of them. Management decided to complete another unrelated piece of software as part of the project, but no one was working on that. She finished by saying that because their senior management was so bad, they'd given up and decided to go with the flow and not really do anything. Let me reiterate: my friend is smart, really smart, really motivated, very clever, and I have a heap of time for them. But what's happened? They're not a slacker or a shirker and they generally have a very solid work ethic.

I was going to use this anecdote to go on about how bad management was and why this type of managment should be taken out back and shot and all of that good stuff, when I was invited to after conference drinks with my friend and a couple of her friends from the same company who were over in New Zealand at the same conference.

Seeing them interact and hearing them talk derogatorily and with bitterness about the project, its product, and their company, I realized that despite that each of these people probably had an average IQ higher than yours and mine put together, they sounded just like the management they were criticizing—like they were running the company despite (or more precisely to spite) management's efforts. They'd been infected by some terminal malaise, had given up fighting a long time ago, and were now so ingrained in the unhealthy balance of their company that they had become very much part of the problem.

So the answer to my question, "What's happened?" wasn't that bad management sapped this person's will to live (which can and probably did happen), but by being complicit and "taking it" every day of their working lives up till that point, the individual had helped their management do it to them, were now fully fledged "management" themselves, and as accountable for their project failures as the management the friends had been slagging off.

I later asked my friend why she didn't leave the company and go work for someone else. They became vague and a little distracted, mentioning something about their kids and spouse, having to work in a particular location, and generally tried to side step the question. As we've known each other for years, I pressed her by saying it sounded like she'd given up and that basically she didn't want to change even given an intellect that would flame Einstein.

She responded directly, asked me for another drink, and then said that (in summary) it was safer—in terms of family—not to risk a move to another company and the potential weeks or months without a salary to stay at their present organisation. The fix for her was just too great an effort to undertake. She definitely understood that it was this decision that was adding to the problems the company's projects had. My suggestion for her to step up into a management position to get things back on track just initiated her wry, "there'd be no point" smile.

But why was such a large project running without a PM? There's a raft of problems occurring in this organization that has nothing to do with software or management (or for that matter, project management).

As I stated at the beginning, project success revolves around people, not "bad management" or bad process, events, or even bad planning. Part of a PM's job is to figure out who is working for them and what the people working for them are truly motivated by. Just what is happening in the organisation in which he or she is trying to manage projects? In the IT project space, people's real motivations are as complex and abstract as in other industries and have nothing to do with engagement or the company's mission statement.

Engagement

I admit that this section is like shooting fish in a barrel. HR theories are still deeply conflicted and yet to reach their foundation synthesis. A fair comment? I think so. For me, I'm neither a "hard" nor "soft" approach advocate, but I definitely veer towards the pluralist theory in which management and employee needs and goals can be and are often in conflict and with transparency added so that everyone gets to make decisions based on good information. This is directly opposed to the "mushroom principle."4 Fundamentally, I have an (apparently) cold and cynical view on what really motivates people. While it might not be completely correct for project management where relatively short bursts of high performance are needed, it's perhaps a better form of HR guidance than all this PC nonsense growing through the cracks of present day HR theory.

Cracking right along, I would say motivators for employees and contractors alike are at worst self-preservation orientated and at best self-advancement orientated from top to bottom; there doesn't seem to be anything else. The Maslow model stands up by itself, but I doubt whether anything past the physiological level is really being met by our organisations. How can it be when, from the safety level upwards, it's really up to the individual to obtain or attain it? In fact, we could go as far as to say that engagement models are a direct threat to an individual's ability to attain fulfilment at these levels—especially safety. Personal fulfilment may be placed on hold for pro-tracted periods of time like my friend's case above. Their company had been through so many middle managers and HR drives over the years that the long-term serving employees there simply ignored them or sabotaged them!

It seems old management theory still stands; an organisation can-not really affect their employees' engagement unless the employee allows them to. The power lies with the employee, not the manager, and even then the employee is only rearranging their internal moti-vators to make whatever—erm, had an expletive here originally—is being sold to them, fit with their own outlook and personal goals. So the employee is *not* adopting the decree, instruction, or engage-ment at a primary level or at all, but just modelling compliance to maintain the reason they are there in the first place, which is money. Let's face it; every new engagement exercise we initiate is moving our employees' cheese.

---

4 Mushroom Principle for those who aren't aware of it states that, like mushrooms, staff should be and are "kept in the dark and fed bullshit" as a management style.

The boiled-down view here is we give employees (I'll include contractors as employees in this section) money and money meets their
ability to satisfy their basic needs and support their higher needs.
Anything else, like fulfilment at a higher level, is a personal thing for
the employee and driven by the foundation of our basic agreement
with them, which is "you work I give money" whether this is in our
organisation or someone else's!

So, as "bad management" not only are we not affecting a change in
the employee, which will ensure engagement, but the employees—
whether they are aware of it or not—are only making a relatively
superficial rearrangement of internal motivators to fit whatever
fresh hell we just dumped on them match their primary motivator.
Ironically, employees have probably just switched from self-advancement to self-preservation because of our interference. How demoralising must it be for an employee to be asked to give feedback on
management without a) a section in which to respond that they
think management really sucks (in other words honestly and directly)
without fear of reprisal and b) no real change occurs as a result of
that feedback.

The more we keep thrusting this engagement, feedback, and ad
nauseum rubbish on employees, the more our goals will become
misaligned with theirs and the more disaffected our employees will
become until they become disgruntled. We won't know about that
until it's too late, if ever, and we will not be able to control it. This is
one of the reasons, I think, for the gaping rifts between management and employee. It keeps getting wider until restructure happens
and the employee leaves or is fired or we start on another round
of time and money-wasting engagement and feedback. Perhaps
restructures are really a symptom resulting from the corporate management body forgetting the primary relationship with their staff
and filling the leadership space with so-called "bad management" to
treat the symptom and not the cause.

It is common nowadays to go into an organisation to complete project management activities and walk straight into a restructure, the tail of one, or an up-in-coming one where sourcing skilled and experienced staff in that organisation's business or technology intellectual property (IP) becomes a nightmare of social navigation and "treading on eggshells." Direction from management is at best vague and at worst some form of misdirection—especially if they are up for the chop as well.

Project management in these environments has little to do with good process and a lot to do with the ability to ride the waves of restructure change and establish the impacts of them and then communicate these back to the so called "bad management" that hired us. This is often a message that the work they wanted done shouldn't be completed until the restructure and its impacts are complete; this will mean we (as contract PMs) shouldn't and won't get paid for it. We don't hide this and soldier on just because it keeps us in work!

Environmental influences around active employee engagement activities and restructures should not be underestimated in their ability to totally negate the business need for a project and to stuff up projects. We can lead a horse to water but we can't make project resources perform in line with scope, cost, time, and to quality if their own management has moved their cheese. This brings us nicely to the next section, which takes a wider view about the environment in which we practice project management.

PS: About six months after our conversation, I heard that my friend finished the project by driving it almost single handedly to completion. Aw! A happy ending? Did they become so very inspired in talking about the project that they gathered up their gumption and finished things for the sake of their company? No. They just became so frustrated with the project and company and got it over with so that they could go do something else in the company with less stress and expectations of performance (a summary of their words).

PPS: Two months after I heard the project was complete, I then heard the company view was that the project was not really finished and they've now sought international help to complete the software build. My friend is now back on the resurrected project reporting to a project manager they like.

The Skin of Mediocrity

*I have of late—but
wherefore I know not—lost all my mirth, forgone all
custom of exercises; and indeed it goes so heavily
with my disposition that this goodly frame, the
earth, seems to me a sterile promontory, this most
excellent canopy, the air, look you, this brave
o'erhanging firmament, this majestical roof fretted
with golden fire, why, it appears no other thing to
me than a foul and pestilent congregation of vapours..*

Hamlet: Act II, scene 2

Democracy is cool, until something more enlightened comes along that supports freedom, individuality, and individual, social, and national well-being better than democracy, it'll be the coolest form of government ever. It's been around for ages, which is cool in itself; anything with the kind of staying power that democracy has must have something going for it, especially when it comes to laying a foundation for a "civilized" society. But in its present form it does bring along with it some certain, inherent constraints that filter through any society fortunate enough to be underneath its great and protective arms.

Arrrgh barbarians! A cry not heard for millennia. Arrrgh, I'm being oppressed by a feudal lord! Again, this hasn't been heard in truly democratic countries for centuries outside of S&M sessions and there's a good reason for this. Democracy is our savior and pro-tector. It cradles the adoptive society within a set of attitudes and behaviors for interactions not only for its government but also for all those living within that society. It has a divide, a skin if you like, with everything and everyone behind that skin safely nuzzling on democracy's milk and everything on the other side in an "unmanaged" state.

If we were bold enough or daring enough to walk right up to that skin with the intention of pushing through it when we were about to take our last step, democracy would kindly flash a warning sign up saying, "Here be dragons!" This would remind us that once we take that last step, outside the skin is a harsh and barbaric world of deeply mind-altering anarchic difference. Our steps beyond that point will most likely be numbered. And then, as we push our foot through the skin, democracy would once again try to gently but firmly prevent us from going by providing the final "system message" of sanity and decency we would see if we continued. I'm sure it would say something like this "Warning! You are now leaving democracy. Your health and well-being will not be supported in an unmanaged environment. Do you wish to continue? OK. Cancel."

What if we continued? Well then it's all up to us, literally. There are no laws, no rules, no organisations, nothing we would find at all familiar or be able to fall back on if times got tough. You see the skin of democracy is not just some arbitrary boundary that comes with its governance; the skin is constructed by the very set of rules and laws that have made a society's particular brand of democracy. This interrelationship, in turn, describes the limits of that society and hence where the skin should lie. For the societal model that is democracy, this distribution describes a bell curve.

This is the perfect time to express a couple of points before going on. Firstly, this will eventually relate to IT and project management. Next, this will not be a sales pitch for pushing the limits or stepping out and becoming an individual; beyond the limit we are talking about is pure badness in which we would have to pack more than our wellingtons and toothbrush to survive. I'm not going to sit here in the comfort of my (often hard fought and hard won by those that have gone before me) democracy (which is currently manifest for me as a perfectly nice, warm and cozy home, in a suburb, in a city which is: not currently on fire, not currently under attack, not riddled with unmanaged disease, and which is functional, clean, and safe enough for me to walk to work—and has such a thing) and write that people should step out of it.

Push the skin to redistribute; yes, that's part of the model. Knock yourself out. But for those secret government agencies that may be reading this and for those individuals not feeling individual enough and who don't understand where the democratic limit is or what it is for (read have no understanding of real anarchy), this particular section will not be a discourse in support of anarchy, subversive practices, and the kind of general silliness that enemies of democracy display.

You see inherent within any bell curve distribution—including democracy's skin— are the retarding agents or factors that form the curve in the first place. One of the wonderful terms we retro-spectively associate to this type of distribution called the law of averages, which in the context of this book could be renamed the "law of average," or more cynically as I like to think of it, the "skin of mediocrity," which unfortunately, if not managed correctly, pro-vides a breeding ground for "bad management" and "bad staff" for that matter.

The pressures that create and maintain a safe haven bell curve in democracy pull, restrain, constrain, and retard the forces that create and forge. By doing so, they result in the force that maintains or sta-bilizes the distribution—society. As such, once the agents of democ-racy are in place, the skin of the distribution becomes self-healing. It has to be; it's another active agent of democracy. We don't want to have to keep establishing the democratic bell curve every time something relatively minor goes wrong or it experiences growth!

But herein lays the main constraint. The result of any bell curve's distribution is the "mass" of the population that gorgeously bloats into a bump of total "averageness." This includes performance or the ability to perform—in the context of IT projects.

Don't get angry at me for saying it: management theory has been here before me stating that human performance across any group of individuals is always normalized. Don't confuse any of this with a value judgment of human worth. I just want to lay out some mechanisms that exist within our society so that we can map them into certain structures within which most of us undertake IT project management.

We also need to understand that our democratic parent is a mother and she gives birth to replicas of herself in all our structures throughout our society. Specifically, she has birthed the institution, the organisation, the department, and supported the rise of the independent or private corporation. Each of these operational structures hides a secret. They aren't exact replicas of democracy nor do they have to be, to be fair. They only have to operate within its skin. They are, however, at best Shakespearian Roman senates (of varying corruptness) and at worst tragedies of royal proportions; although surrounded and cushioned by the bosom of mother democracy, they are still fraught with all the dangers of the senate and the royal household.

Why wouldn't they be? These structures operate under a double bind of averageness—the overall bell curve of democracy constraining the skin of mediocrity and mimicking democracy under their own structures, thinly veiling dictatorships, despots, communist pods, kangaroo courts, and senates of ultimate power. All support their own, self-healing skin of mediocrity no matter what organizational external raison d'etre is pushed and accepted publically.

In fact, the closer we look at any organisation of the twenty-first century, applying the analogies of the comic and tragic roman senate and the dramas of royal households from Shakespearian jaunts, the weirder they get, until their existence becomes almost inane, and their efforts sometimes puerile. Seriously—360 degree feedback sessions? Come on! Just get back to work and actually govern and measure the performance of those working for us in return for hard cash! Oops...too much? OK, off my high horse now. These organizational structures are perfect hiding places for "bad management" and "bad staff." However, let's define these terms here in light of this section.

What we are really saying is that some roles require more of a performance-based acumen but have been staffed with those without the capability to fulfill them, giving rise to "bad" management and staff. We see this in project management in people who need the power a formal authority grants them, which they could never muster from their personal power. Bad management and staff run riot with budgets and resources and compound the problem by hiring other people based on the limits of their skills, experience, and understanding—not because they are "bad" but because they are in positions where they are out of their depth.

Average management and staff within these structures will flourish, protected by the very retarding and self-healing forces that give rise to stability within those structures in the first place. They will then form small corrupt kingdoms, principalities and micro-senates manipulating the very rules set up to protect this from happening.

But wait; there's more. Perhaps it's always been this way, but the advent of the information age we are surrounded by has provided the tools to elevate almost every human being to be "connected" to great swags of information. While the bell curve hasn't changed, the occupations of those within it have. Automation has led to more service than production. But running this information age and its automation, especially considering the immaturity of the technology supporting it and the understanding of it (as evident by the continued rate of change and continually reforming maturity curve in IT) seems to require a shift along the x performance axis that is just not occurring. Organisations simply cannot afford to have "average" staff and management fulfill these roles any more.

This brings me to the actual focus of this section; it is these environments we actually face as project managers in IT.

We need to acknowledge that IT projects have a higher requirement for performance-based staff, both from a technical point of view and a practice point of view. Projects have to deliver things. They have to do so in a prescribed amount of time and money, and to a pretty rigorous set of quality. Even if this is inversely evident, only at the end of an IT project when the system fails because of a lack of well-defined requirements and acceptance criteria up front. It is precisely the wrong area to let the law of average place people in such roles. It is wrong to let vague and loose recruitment processes staff projects without those running the processes having the ability to identify what performance is required.

Also, we as PMs need to assess the particular brand of bell curve we are heading into. Is there a "king" somewhere making all the real calls? If so, who are they and how are they hiding this well of power from their management and staff? Who owns the senate and which senator are we working for?

We have to find the boundaries for what can and can't be done, fixed, or changed in the environment we are actually facing—and I don't mean the one that we all assume is a democracy, full of love and respect and ikkle wittle fluffy bunnies. We then have to make decisions based on this information. How far has the rot set in, if at all? Has any project got a real chance for success in the environment we are facing? Remember organizational structures are sold as democracies, or part of one, but in reality they won't be. There will be fiefdoms and senates throughout the organisation that we need to effect delivery in. Whose toes will we tread on if we're successful?

Finally, we must acknowledge that the structures we call programmes, projects, work streams, and governance, are in fact further pseudo-replicas of the mother democracy cradling the organisation we are operating within. In effect, these structures are not remotely democratic; they are and must be dictatorships within a democracy, with one person making the call. A less emotive way of expressing this would be to say that there should be a consul in every IT project.

Instead of leading a legion to effect conquering and quelling on behalf of the senate and Caesar, as they did in Roman times, the consul leads a team to effect delivery of agreed system and platform changes. The key question in any IT project is who is the consul? The project manager, the project executive, or someone else?

Further, our project structures (and environments they exist within) lend themselves naturally to the same forces of average that have produced and populated their structures in the first place. If we are not extremely mindful, the law of average will pour through our carefully laid plans and processes as soon as we take our eye—and hence attention—off of it.

Bad Behavior

What a piece of work is a man! how noble in reason! how infinite in faculty! in form and moving how express and admirable! in action how like an angel! in apprehension how like a god! the beauty of the world! the paragon of animals! And yet, to me, what is this quintessence of dust? man delights not me: no, nor woman neither, though by our smiling you seem to say so.
Hamlet: Act II, scene 2

In recent years I've had the misfortune to witness the behaviors outlined in this section every working day—sometimes even directed at me. It used to be a rare occurrence for certain people that were known for it. I'm not talking about the occasional heated debate I would be able to understand and accept. Even the occasional swear word thrown in for emphasis or from sheer frustration I can accept, but the extent and frequency of the behaviors I witnessed returning to IT project management was one of the main reasons I started writing this book. This is a reminder that the following types of behavior are unacceptable in a professional workplace.

- Yelling or firing attacks at an individual until he or she is speechless, oppressed, and/or in tears
- Bullying by withholding information, steering conversations, demoralising remarks, snide looks, never putting instructions or agreements in writing, and creating "sides" with peers
- Backstabbing
- Rumor mongering
- Lying
- Imposing the impossible on an individual
- Setting others up to fail
- Not allowing an individual to finish what he or she is saying
- Racism, sexism, ageism, and homophobia
- Using or hiding behind formal authority and senior associations that prevent other bad behaviors from being seen or resolved
- Scapegoating when things have gone wrong—including unreasonably threatening termination
- Playing the player and not the ball (directing criticism at a person personally or setting someone else up to take the blame)
- Senior and exec staff not stopping this behavior!

It's got me thinking, where do these behaviors really come from and what could be done about it? In regards to the latter—nothing; there is nothing I can do from pages of this book to prevent this behavior from occurring. There is no idealistic, happy world of resolution that can be magically applied. What I can do is—political correctness aside—explain exactly where this behavior comes from.

It doesn't boil down to one type of person. It boils down to all types of people in specific situations. We all need to see this behavior for what it is; the person displaying it is struggling in their job and probably their life because they

- Feel out of their depth
- Don't actually understand what their job entails
- Have failed to manage their part
- Feel out of control
- Haven't developed past the "terrible tantrum" phase from their childhood when dealing with stressful situations (or have regressed into it)
- Never evolved past a teenage level of social interaction (or have regressed into it)

Also, IT PMs need to understand that the reason these bad behaviors are so prevalent is because of that paragraph I wrote regarding what makes IT projects fail in the Background and Introduction section. There are so many people in IT project management that do not know what their jobs are nor do they have the required skills and experience to do them. This means that most are feeling out of control, and this is a prerequisite to all the not so nice behaviors we see.

This does extend both ways from a project management level, downwards into the team, and upwards into senior and exec management. Upwards is perhaps worse because managers who feel this way will not do anything about those staff displaying the behavior underneath their position because they are displaying it themselves; managers actually breed a culture of this behavior in their staff and we as IT PMs face this type of behavior every day.

As an IT PM, we need to understand that

- The person displaying this behavior is doing so because of the reasons in the previous list
- The person is having a fear-based reaction that has triggered a "flight or fight" mechanism
- That this behavior is ultimately rooted in following fears:
    - The fear of death (being fired. Yep, go figure!)
    - The fear of not being good enough
    - The fear of not being accepted
    - The fear of being ostracized
    - The fear of being ridiculed or publically shamed
    - The fear of being unloved and unlovable (Yes, I know this is gooey emotional stuff—get over it)
- The person is not able to differentiate between what is happening at a professional level and what they feel is happening to them—internally (see list of fears above)

These behaviors are pure reaction and so deeply rooted that they will stop at almost nothing to cover themselves. The people displaying them have such a dearth of skills and experience appropriate for their jobs that this has become a default state for them from which to operate. They have developed complex coping strategies internally to help deal with the pressures this situation brings. The behaviors we see are the "tip of the iceberg" for what's going on underneath. Strategies include both knowing how to hide behind and work the system (rather than actually doing any work), how to play infant level social games, and how to put vast amounts of energy into implementing these strategies because they are basically a toddler in an adult's body. They have reverted to that state because of stress. Because they are in a position of power in an adult situation, they will throw the unwary and throw others under the bus.

This is what is causing the bad behavior we see around us. The problem for us is that it's unethical if we play on the fears of these people to our advantage or set them up to self-implode by using those fears against them. I am told that both things are surprisingly easy to do, but it would make us very bad people if we used this knowledge against our colleagues displaying the behaviors above.

Also, we need to acknowledge that a code of conduct is only good until it is broken. Good luck actually getting anything done about rectifying a situation where code has been broken and bad behavior is happening—especially if it's the most senior member in the group to have signed the code displaying the behavior. The real value of the codes of conduct is not in managing and agreeing conduct, but in identifying people in this unfortunate situation who will likely play up on our projects.

A client once required a code of conduct for their new project. They hadn't asked for one, but their behavior prompted me to write one. I was able to figure out several things before tabling the code. When I tabled the code formally, I already expected them to react strongly. If they rejected it, then it was time for me to move on and excuse myself immediately (without causing a threat to the project, if possible). If they accepted it, those that had reacted against it the strongest would be the ones to watch out for. I had already identified that the person at the top of the programme hierarchy was one of those people, so the code wouldn't last long and they would expect not to be held to the code. If they reacted and I said the code was a common PMI practice and recommended it be implmeneted, they would make some excuse not to adopt it. They didn't accept the code and actually quoted that they were PRINCE2 and so PMI tools weren't appropriate.

Now this is the kind of tool PMs in IT really need—PMs don't need a code of ethics that only PMI members and accredited professionals sign. In practice (while I support our PMI code fully), it's just not enough. We need to arm PMs with the kind of tools like "note the reaction to codes of conduct to decide whether or not we wish to stay in a job/contract/position." This will actually make PMs more successful and happier in their profession.

There's another angle we need to be aware of: Project management is and should be black and white. If we come along and try implementing a good, transparent project management process, we will in fact be in direct conflict with the people displaying or prone to this behavior. Here's a good example:

A good friend of mine was hired by an outsourcing company as a PM for one of the company's larger clients. Their job was to reestablish basic project practice in the client's project because the outsourcing company's last PM had gone "feral." The client's project executive also had a penchant for pointing fingers, yelling, and changing their mind every week about scope (this is not an exaggeration—I peer reviewed the scope findings of my friend's project forensics), and then expecting the outsourcing company to wear it; some good practice was definitely called for. The whole situation "smelt bad" to my jaded nose, and I warned my friend not to continue in the job, but they graciously refused to take my advice.

Eight weeks into the contract, my friend was hauled through the client's HR system for bullying (seriously) when the project exec lodged a formal complaint against my friend for putting basic project management processes in place! Fortunately my friend and the hiring company had previously agreed just how bad things were. They got the company's backing to proceed and agree that only basic project practice would be put in place. My friend was warned about their behavior and was let off with a threat about being taken off the account. Can you believe that?

Turns out the project exec in question had even pressured the outsourcing company's own project team who were on-site in an effort to get them to speak against my friend. The team was literally cornered after work when no one was around and pressured to speak against my friend, which of course they didn't, as my friend is a good PM and had quickly won favor with the team. The exec was so threatened, he did not think twice about crossing the accepted social behavior line or stumbling his way across the illegal line. I'm sorry, but what a douchebag!

My friend was shaken about this and what it meant to our profession. You see, this situation doesn't just lie within the bounds of that project. Upon further probing for information from my friend, it became evident that the complaint only got to the HR stage because the exec and his peer responsible for conduct in their particular group both reported to the same boss. The exec was such a bully that his peer was too scared to go against his colleague in front of his boss and accuse him of "bad behavior" for fear of reprisals. So the outsourcing company and my friend wore it.

Personally, I would have expected the outsourcing company to stand up for the PM they'd hired and take the brunt of the full force, excusing my friend from actually having to go through the HR process. But (and it's a big but), the outsourcing company was so scared about damaging the account that they had my friend answer the complaints. At least they went with him and supported him through it, but that's not really the point though, is it?

The processes my friend tried to put into place were the most basic of decision tracking and forecasting, but it showed up the project exec and his erratic behaviors, plain and simple. This is not the worst story I have either; it's just one of the worst ones I have professional experience with.

Personally, I could go on about witnessing the screaming matches, personal attacks, ambushes, and the pure petty-minded, underdeveloped unreasonableness my colleagues and I have witnessed.

Like the operational manager who had eight different people from different organisations, including his own, gently explain to him why a project would take nine months, who then erupted with a mouthful of expletives and made everyone do it in six months upon the risk of dismissal. It took nine months but cost more than originally planned because of the added and unreasonable time pressures and rescheduling required. It put everyone under a lot of stress.

Or the PMO manager who hired me to fire someone they didn't like, there was no other reason and no other reasoning to be found. I had to report that the targeted person in question was doing an OK job and then face a lecture on how bad I was at my job for not "joining in the manager's club."

Or the time a manager of mine accidentally showed up our CIO in front of their peers (I like to think of it this way "you made me look stupid" paraphrasing the CIO. No, you did that perfectly well on your own without any help from us), we all heard the screaming coming from his office, and my manager didn't last the week before the CIO fired them—which was a pity because the manager was making some really healthy changes.

The thing that has changed here over the years is that, while we were "growing up" in our professions, excuses were being used around us that enabled this behavior. We were often told that it was just the way of things and that we didn't understand because we were so young and inexperienced. Well, we've stuck around and now we're heading into "grumpy old men and women" territory ourselves with enough seniority. We are reaching and surpassing the levels of those that have held these attitudes. Now, as an experienced and senior manager, I am simply going to say that bad behavior is just unacceptable; there is never a good excuse for it. It is not "the way of things" but it is maintained by people too scared or apathetic to do anything about it.

In the instances of bad behavior I have to deal with or review, I often I find that it is in fact one of those times that it is management's fault because it's clear the person displaying the behavior is out of their depth or struggling without the right skills and experience and the behavior is a reaction to it. Putting this person in the role in the first place was a management mistake. Leaving someone in this position without support after you've been told that they are struggling is another mistake. To be clear, I am talking right up into CIO level and beyond—the people who display the behavior and the people who have the responsibility to resolve it.

If you're still thinking *No really, that's just the way it is in real life*, then again you're enabling the situation and part of the problem—no excuses.

Projects in General

Project Management is Cool

I saw a truck recently that read on its side, "Your project is safe with us." I thought, *Awesome! Maybe they've got some good project managers and processes we can apply in IT.* But no, on closer inspection I found it was for an office relocation service. Obviously each office relocation is treated as a project, which is all well and good, but it got me thinking. It seems that everything is a project these days and everyone has the title project manager, and we can see why.

Project managers are cool; they get things done! They're the ones in control, in charge and up front. They are the new sales reps of the '70s and '80s, the new IT geeks of the '90s (can you remember the snide and condescending "I'm in IT" comments. Awesome, so are we, only we're good at it you numpty). They are the latest in corporate coolness in the ever-growing awareness and trend in project management within the corporate structures of the early twenty-first century.

Project managers are in fact the green berets of the corporate world and projects are the Special Operations missions, and with good reason.

A project is the exact opposite of the day-to-day grind; a project is the epitome of everything that's not regular, routine, boring, staid, and dreary. Hence, anyone who runs one of these babies gets the label of "unique and groovy" rubbing off on them.

That's why the words "project" and title project manager are the latest buzz words to drop into a conversation if we want to appear suave and sophisticated. "Oh yea, I'm on a project at the moment." (Read: it's so much more sexy than your day-to-day work and why yes, I am indeed a complete idiot). "It's got a huge budget," (Read: I have no idea what it's about or what I'm doing, but the money is disappearing faster than the glaciers. Someone should do something about it), "and they've asked me to step up and manage it." (Read: this request alone immediately makes me fit for a project management role, they wouldn't have asked me to fill the role otherwise!) "Wanna come back to my house and see my Gannt chart?"

Unfortunately, as people want to do, this particular bandwagon has not so much been jumped on as been run at full tilt and leapt on by every nut job who feels inadequate in corporate social situations and is dissatisfied with their previous profession (which they probably can't do well anyway). Therein lies the problem.

Project management is an applied practice like a profession. It's not something we move into for a while. It's not something we just pick up because our day job has provided us with the skills. It's not a reward for excellence in another position. It's not something we can do successfully without appropriate training. It's not something we can successfully practice unless we have an active peer network and mentors, constantly develop our understanding about it, and practice it using the culmination of these prerequisites; and let's be absolutely clear here, the attendance and the successful passing of the PRINCE2 Foundation and Practitioner qualifications or PMI's PMP does not make us a project manager either! It just makes us familiar with practicing the PRINCE2 methodology and using the PMBOK Guide. There's much more to project management than that!

But no, now everyone is a project manager from the receptionist arranging that office move who puts project manager in her CV, to the (albeit senior) engineer who's now running that upgrade project for us because it didn't really warrant a (real) project manager. In this sense we are all project managers.

As a profession we don't help ourselves either. We have anecdotes and analogies that we use when explaining what a project is to novices and how it equates to other things in our lives, such as "If you've planned and taken a holiday, then you've managed a project!" Note the exclamation mark because when speaking that sentence, we PMs do in fact inflect strongly at the end of it to prove the point that project management can be as simple as that. Argh! While I appreciate this analogy within a training context and at face value while coaching (smiley face on), many people have run this particular ball out of the stadium.

Now everyone's a project manager and this understanding has been taken literally by people who have done nothing else remotely like project management with the exception of planning a holiday. These "project managers" are now fronting up for work and calling themselves PMs. But they do not have the prerequisite experience, support, and qualifications. Even worse, hiring managers in the same category—without the prerequisites above multiplied by seniority—continue to hire these people as PMs.

First of all, this rush of perhaps enthusiastic yet challenged project managers into the practice dilutes the effectiveness of the archetypal project manager and what a project manager actually is. This then feeds the second issue, which is an ever-growing mistrust of project managers and projects, especially in IT. This is because so many people (who aren't project managers) are doing such a poor job of it and costing corporates millions of dollars; those around them equate their poor performance to the professional project manager.

Real project management is challenging work. It requires fortitude of spirit, a multifaceted intellect, and an emotional development akin to self-actualization to abstract and manage the multidimensional matrix of time-bound, cost-bound, thing-bound interrelated event spaces which define a project—while at the same time also managing multiple, complex, interrelated, social interactions and relationships, with the PM at the focal point of all of these aspects.

Like a colleague of mine once said shortly before being fired (not by me), "I hate this! I feel like I'm in the middle of everything!" That's pretty much a good definition of a project manager's job! Project management is a profession where we cannot hide. We either get done the thing we started out doing or it's visible to everyone that we haven't, why we haven't, and how badly we haven't. And if we get that thing done, it's visible how well we managed it.

Therein lays the twisted, demented, but glorious irony to all this project management buzz. People who expect a free ride to popularity as a PM and who fail to manage the most basic of project processes—causing the project failures we are experiencing—will get exposed eventually. Unfortunately for the project sponsors, executives, and real-life professional project managers, the damage will have been done.

Myth of the Percentage PM

Thirty percent. That's how much (on top of a technical budget) we should allow for project management costs. Seriously, this is a "methodology" that is used all too frequently to estimate or limit the project management effort on IT projects. Sometimes it's 15 percent or 20 percent. Still, this approach for estimating a project manager's time on any given IT project is mind-numbingly dangerous.

The approaches, durations, and project management needs on any given IT project are as different to each other as apples from pears, and will be specific to each and every project. Even common sense tells us that on some projects, and definitely some phases of a project, a project manager can be part time; or that in some really complex or larger projects with multiple work streams, there may be a need for more than one project manager. These facts alone will skew the "30 percent" on one project to the next.

What if there are only two resources required and no hardware procurement on one nine month project, and yet on another there is significant hardware investment needed and a team of twenty, across the same period? The 30 percent may be all that's need for the first. And for the second? Well we've (hopefully) significantly overestimated the project management effort required. What if some project is so complex that it had only one resource at any one time working on it, but yet for the duration requires the attention and administration of a fulltime project manager? Even a generalization or hindsight application of statistical data across a portfolio review for a given period (even if it does come out at around 30 percent) is not the way to apply the "similar project" estimating technique for the next project we take on.

Individual projects, when assessed for outturn will not always be any-where close to 30 percent project management effort—or any other "rule of thumb" percentage. We have to apply breakdowns for effort across all roles, especially project managers, and do so by assessing the risk, duration, scope boundary, overhead/reporting requirements, and even the nature of the undertaking in question before we can say how big a project manager's role will be on any given project.

So why do this? It's not savvy or sophisticated. It's not an accepted project management technique. It's costing us money and causing us discomfort. Stop it! This is a line management mistake—and that's not a criticism. There is a reason PMI developed the PMBOK® Guide and the OCG adopted and then developed further PRINCE2 (and both their relative programme and portfolio efforts).

Project management is different than line management. We can't use the same processes to plan, estimate, or control portfolios (projects), or estimate their health as we do for line management areas. The inherent unstable and unknown nature of projects, and their management, means that a period-based forecast or estimate focusing on fixed expenses and overheads for the delivery or maintenance of repeatable services (plus a profit margin if appropriate) is not an appropriate approach for the overall management estimates of projects.

If we're in ultimate control of a portfolio or programme of work and have no experience with (or at least are not familiar with) the associated management techniques, we will be unable to efficiently manage that portfolio or programme using only line management techniques. In fact, we may run them into the ground or not remotely achieve the goals or realize the benefits of those undertakenings.

The international project management bodies are not trying to pull the wool over our eyes. It's not some way to charge us more for project management or keep us guessing and on the back foot. It's just the nature of a project that we will not know the exact total cost of it until it's finished—and no one is spending any time on it.

If a project manager approaches us with a project estimate with a 25 percent range during the initiation stage of a project, or a 10 percent ranged forecast once the project is underway, this isn't because they're an idiot or bad at their job and can't give us an exact figure; in fact, the exact opposite is true. This person knows that things will change before the end of the project. We should count ourselves lucky we have them. It's to our advantage to run projects as projects and to understand the general approaches to project management for our level. It's a pay as we go, get-what-we-pay-for approach. We couldn't want for a better approach for something as changeable as projects! It's a way of managing an entire raft of new interdependent events—events that have only come into being because we asked for something additional to happen outside of normal operations.

Many of these events will not have occurred before. Little will be known about them, apart from what project managers can see by using the accepted project management techniques.

It's the exact opposite of knowing and predicting a series of expected or bound events (resulting in service level agreements (SLAs) for instance) and having reaction plans for them, as we do for the majority of IT services. It's the exact opposite of fixing costs for infrastructure across a period of time because we know what we want and have in our environments when we start the forecast.

Half the problem—which I tackle in detail in the last section of this book—is that our mistrust of project management in IT, and hence a preference to stick with what we know (line practices) is because of that claim I made in that paragraph at the beginning of the book. Our trust in projects and project management in IT is shot through, but it can be fixed and we should not throw the baby out with the bathwater, or in other words ditch good project practices because our PMs and PMOs have burned us in the past.

In Name Only

Five months after the Christchurch February 22 earthquake in 2011, I moved to my nation's capital, Wellington (which houses the majority of our government offices) to find work; the earthquake literally gutted the contract market for IT PMs in Christchurch as it gutted Christchurch itself.

From the get-go people started quoting PRINCE2 at me during interviews. It was hard enough that I had to attend interviews for the first time in years because the luxury and comfort of being known and trusted in another smaller city didn't really count for much. But to have this PRINCE2 thing landed on me like I was a substandard project manager was not a great feeling.

And it was everywhere. "We're PRINCE2 here," came from vendors and government organizations alike. "If you want to work in this town you'll have to become PRINCE2 certified." This went on as contracts and clients progressed.

To my undying shame, I was not PRINCE2 at all. I'd happily and successfully used management stages and gates before as an addition to monitoring and controlling decision making and readiness when working in a PMBOK based PMO, but really I didn't know the first thing about PRINCE2 itself.

As time went on, these almost accusatory references (and I admit the associated pressure and implications) were becoming annoying. People were getting away with things because of my lack of PRINCE2 knowledge, trying to pull the wool over my eyes. "Oh no, that's PRINCE2," indicating that I was at some significant deficit because of my lack of certification.

So, as I needed to fulfill my quotient of professional development units for my ongoing PMP requirements, and attending PRINCE2 would give me a good selling point for the city I was living in, I decided to take my foundation and practitioner exams and see what all this PRINCE2 stuff was about.

Bingo! First day in (well, in fact the day before when completing prestudy) two things occurred to me. First, PRINCE2 was pretty damn good. It was not to my liking (we fear change) but it was really very sound and useful. Second (and this was confirmed throughout the course), not one person who had quoted PRINCE2 at me since I'd arrived in the city was implementing anything remotely PRINCE2! Have a think about the implications of this for a second.

I talked at length to my tutor about this and he replied with a wry smile and a lesser-known acronym used by real PRINCE2 practitioners. PRINCE2INO (pronounced prince-two-ae-no), or PRINCE2 in name only, is apparently a well-known phenomenon in the PRINCE2 world. This translated into those that say they are actively using PRINCE2 in their work, but are really only doing what I've described in the "What IT Project Management really is" sections.

It was not even that those who had quoted PRINCE2 at me had mistaken tailoring for only using bits of PRINCE2—that's right we have to use all of it. Every process and every activity and product needs some treatment in an implementation and it needs to be tailored to the maturity, capability, and risk appetite of the organisation we are in; it was that no one was doing anything remotely like the specification of PRINCE2 project management.

I've witnessed similar things before on a more individual scale with PMP holders and the PMBOK® Guide. Some hold the qualifications but not employing a single thing from the PMBOK® Guide and sell themselves as "PMBOK practitioners." I had even experienced a similar 'in name only' situation in PMOs that had adopted the PMBOK® Guide as a basis but were really still maturing with their implementation (see I can be nice), but the extent of people saying they were implementing PRINCE2 but weren't actually implementing it was incredible.

Like SCRUM and the PMBOK® Guide, the adoption of PRINCE2 as part of project management standards for an organisation is as much about cultural change and a change in project management maturity as it is practice and process. To have so many people quoting the name PRINCE2 at me for months but not walking the talk was and is truly outstanding.

It got me all riled up. I still feel the need to write and complain to someone, anyone! My local MP? The prime minister? The president of the United States? Someone somewhere has to do something![5] Oh dear. I just realized I'm turning into one of those grumpy old men that actually write and complain about breaches in broadcasting standards.

Just what is going on in the world of IT project management? And don't lay it on the government sector or those who mandate or strongly suggest the use of PRINCE2; I've worked for government PMOs that would run circles around some private sector equivalents.

But as I said above, think about the implications: standards where there aren't any, practices in name only, assurance to a high level within an organisation when there is nothing to base that assurance on. The issue here stripes through just about every other section I've written so far and lands squarely in the responsibility of management.

Delivery, practice, programme, project and portfolio managers: We can't afford to have portfolios, programmes, and projects as complex as our IT initiatives running to practice standards in name only; if we're holding these positions we need to understand and get qualified in the standards our professional area is meant to work to and become the force to implement and maintain them.

Execs and board members: if our organisations quote project management standards and practices to us in reports and reviews, especially when they are asking for money, we need to seriously question these assertions and be in a position to gauge whether they are true or not. If you read the project selection section of this book you'll understand that it's at this point in their lifecycle when IT projects

---

5 But the one thing I can't do is write to the professional governing body of project management in my country (or any other)—because there isn't one! Is it really any wonder we are in this state?

really fail. Just keep thinking to yourself those two terrifying words: sunk cost.

Still, a refreshing bonus for me is that now that I'm a certified practitioner and actively supporting PRINCE2, as much as I do the PMBOK® Guide and SCRUM, people have stopped mentioning PRINCE2 to me. Go figure.

Information Technology—IT

Change and Complexity in IT

The IT projects we deal with change frequently at many levels.

One way of looking at this is simply that it is because projects are change agents. They make change and it's their purpose. As such, in their sphere of operation and their vapour trail they kick up even more change. This change spills over to areas on the very boundary of the changes in scope, which in turn must change to accept the new state the project will bring with its ever growing and tumultuous storm clouds of change.

So hats off to us project managers everywhere; it's a tough job to begin with.

But what if the area we are changing is changing itself while we are trying to complete our project? What if the technical sphere our project is trying to influence is itself in a constant state of flux—its fundamental architecture waving like a pendulum with a 360-degree swing over an entire circle of new ideas and ways of working?

To use an analogy, what if on one Monday in March we built a brick one way, but by the time a Friday at the end of September rolled around, we had to build the same brick another way?

What if the function of every building had to be modified every two years, but the building was so complex that we couldn't rebuild it without listing thousands upon thousands of specific requirements to suit every function for everyone that was going to work or live in it; but this happened on a completely separate axis to the architectural and construction changes occurring at the same time, with independent drivers?

Frankly, what if we had to rebuild a small city and its supporting infrastructure every few years, using techniques, building materials, and approaches that were constantly changing?

The answer is managed chaos—and yet at every level, from micro to macro—this is what we are doing in our IT environments all the time.

It's not too far a stretch to compare a large organisation's total IT environment to a small city and its infrastructure in terms of the level of complexity and interrelatedness for any given supporting system, and the "domain" as an integrated whole. While we maintain our cities over the years, totally replacing road surfaces, completely upgrading water system infrastructure and the like, we don't do all of these things at the same time, within the space of say twenty-four months.

Yet in IT this is exactly what happens. For IT, twenty-four months is a lifetime. In a business' IT environment multiple systems, individually as complex as any single city infrastructure, are upgraded or replaced as our insatiable need for information and performance continues to grow. They are replaced as the infrastructure that they integrate into is being modified or upgraded itself—in many instances completely replaced by something that works in a different way at the same time as management and maintenance principles are also being developed or redeveloped. The move from organisational owned infrastructure and systems to multitenanted cloud-based services is a great example of this.

To top this off, as a society we are still developing the principles and major processes that integrate information technology into our organisations and their operating structures. With so many dimensions of change occurring in and around the technical space itself, as well as the rapid maturity model we are struggling to keep pace with alongside this new technology, managing any project in this environment is going to be hard. No, it's going to be almost impossible.

I have to pay dues now to the thousands of staff in IT keeping our systems afloat. Considering the technical complexity and change occurring in our environments, when we look at IT from this view, it's amazing more catastrophes aren't occurring! If the only cost to our societies and their organisations is the millions of dollars that are going to waste, then in this context, we should count ourselves lucky.

It's not hard to see why there are such wry attitudes from technical staff about management staff in IT when it's a group of technical, and some management staff, who are good at their jobs that actually keep our IT systems working (and use the word "working" in the widest sense possible), despite the efforts of others in the industry and the virulent change occurring within.

It boils down to this: Project management is hard enough, but for IT projects, project management must include the ability to understand, identify, and manage this complex, multi-dimensional change across all levels of the project, general IT technical domain, and in specific technical subject areas. Also, it must include the ability to establish and implement appropriate project management processes while adopting the appropriate technical approach for any given project.

This is why I think project managers in IT must have a technical background in IT to be able to actually manage and steer IT projects successfully. They must be aware of and have experience of these technical dimensions, as well as be experienced in the practices of project management.

Reliance on a primary technical expert—or group of them—will never provide the PM with the understanding that is required to successfully shape and control the path for the project in the first place. Without this technical experience an IT project manager will not be able to control a project in a timely manner— nor will they see issues coming before they arrive as the project progresses. Fundementally a "non-techical" project manager will not be able understand or assess if something has been delivered successfully and completely.

Further, a lack of fully integrated and consolidated programmes of work means that the rapid technical change within our techni- cal environments is largely occurring by itself. It is ocuring as it is needed and sometimes retrospectively—when reacting to critical technical issues. This type of change is always unannounced and definitely not planned for or communicated in advance!

So as an IT PM do not underestimate the severe impact this unplanned, uncommunicated, multidimensional technical change will have on our projects and their carefully laid plans. This type of change has the ability to slice through our projects like someone has taken a can opener to them, causing (sometimes irrecoverable) delays.

From a project control prespective to say this type of techni- cal change causes a complete unravelling of project plans is an understatement.

A Mixed Bag of Nuts—Outsourcing

The first ten years of the turn of the century saw the evolution of outsourcing in one of the many axes of major, nontechnical, swings of the IT pendulum. I can remember a time early in the new millennia when we were all in-house; we were a family with specific roles and knowledge. We mainly got on well together apart from the empire building and massive rifts between IT and business and those that formed between teams. It may be time for the rose-coloured nostalgia glasses to come off.

Projects existed, as did vendors. New systems or network implementations and upgrades were about the only times we saw projects or vendors. Everything that was done was handed over to one of the internal teams and vendors came attached to products.

Then we moved into the brave new world of outsourcing and what a world it was.

For the record, I was never for the offshore outsourcing model to take advantage of cheap labour. It always smelled of "we get what we pay for" and "too good to be true", and it was.

The benefits never really came; we struggled with cultural differences—not just with stereotypical "Indian outsourcers." It turned out that our customers absolutely hated getting a service desk person in a different country asking how the weather was where they were. Also, I was a developer back when outsourcing was emerging and the thing that struck me was languages.

Science now tells us that language and cognisance are (at the very least) closely related, if not interdependent in terms of development. Language development is an influencing factor on cognisance. Well at least that's what it tells us this week. Outsourcing in which one party natively speaks one language and another party speaks another language while developing in yet another language(s) (I think it's fair to count development languages in this mix—they are a collection of symbols and rules, with inherent semantics, used to express concepts and actions) was never going to end well. Both parties had their own native cultural understanding—and mechanisms of understanding—all three languages and the problem space. So when it came to quality expectations, someone in this outsourced arrangement needed to have the ability to understand and manage the overlay at the intersection of all three languages, associated cultures, and understandings.

The last ten years has proven that this intersection management is very hard and simply doesn't happen. In one particular example of offshore outsourcing, this is why I found reviewing over a 150 consecutive "if...then...else" statements in a piece of outsourced code really frustrating. Go figure. It was still a solution that worked, but not one that was elegant, scalable, and easily maintained. The outsourcer was more than a little surprised we were reviewing the code in the first place.

But some outsourcing stuck around and was not always offshore.

In fact, with the advent of ITIL, we outsourced just about everything we could think of. We outsourced server management, network management, boundary management, application management, database management, and even the management of entire environments. We outsourced the management of IT processes as service management, including problem resolution, change, configuration, and capacity management, to name a few. We even outsourced management management—the management of the arrangements of managing the other things. More importantly we outsourced these things to different companies.

And we still think this is OK. We think this is serving us better than anything else we can possibly do. Not sure I'm that comfortable with it because of what it means to IT projects and the additional costs and risks that this brings with it. We now commonly have vast swathes of our horizontal architectures and the infrastructure that implements them managed by different competing companies. It doesn't matter how we view our architecture. As tiers or as services, outsourcing has separated the holistic management of these "vertical" or service-centric slices to the point where remedying a problem or doing anything to them involves multiple vendors and a lot of blank looks.

Why? Because no one vendor understands the whole and no one is managing the in-between bits—the integrative handshake parts of the architecture that make up the steps or jumps between logical (managed) levels. Worse, business responsibility has been outsourced along the way too. The more cynical of us said this would happen way back, resulting in only very small pockets of in-house staff with IP available—if at all. Now IP associated with these slices has been thrown to the wind and is now spread across multiple vendors—vendors we don't use anymore, staff that don't work for us anymore, and individuals holding hegemony over the system in question.

We also need to remember that a corporate entity is responsible for producing profit and staying competitive despite any efforts to form collaborative and supportive working relationships or behaviours between all parties. Isn't it naive of us as customers to continually expect that if we leave the room for a few minutes these different outsourcing guys will play nice? Come on. At worse they're ultimately predators in sheepskins, huddled around our outsourcing table, vying for the scraps that we give them. At best they're good people trying to get work done for us but faced with the reality that at least one other vendor in the mix will be trying to eat another one.

By the time we need to run a project in this environment is it any wonder that, as mentioned earlier, a good amount of project time will be spent maintaining positions whereby the customers or outsourcing companies can point fingers or blame the other parties for delivery and performance problems. A good deal of the rest of the time will be spent trying to track down the integration points and relationships between systems and vertical stacks before we mess with things and following up IP leads with often hostile responses.

Then we get annoyed with our vendors because we let the knowledge slip away from us over the years, and now this information isn't held by one party—if at all.

This is the impact to IT projects by the outsourcing model. When reviewing projects, I commonly find that there's been a good deal of wasted effort and additional project management and technical time spent traversing the outsourced environment in question. No one completely followed up the IP trail because it was too hard and this caused the critical outages and project failure that triggered a review in the first place.

An outsourced and aggregated management role isn't going to solve these problems either. Now we've put one vendor in charge of other competing vendors? We seem, as customers, hell-bent on making it hard on ourselves and our vendors to get anything done efficiently in the project space by setting up in the management space, relationships, and processes that conflict with project management. As if at some point in the outsourcing past we lost control of the environment in a bad-way (i.e., we let our business down by trying to farm out to vendors the ultimate responsibility we (still) have to provide information technology for the business' consumption—vendors who, over time, have been swapped out because of poor performance or because of a change of the IT management or because they were too expensive.

This brings me to the next section. Caught up in this outsourcing drama and related to the comments in the line management section above are "pencil-sharpening" exercises we expose our vendors to in the project space if they are providing management services as well as project services.

A Conflict of Interest?

As customers, I think we're cruel to our outsourcing vendors, especially if they are providing us with project and management services.

Why? Because the very nature of what they are providing in management services are not unique, are repeatable, and are not time constrained services (in terms of terminal delivery of things and stuff, so SLA behavior aside). These services are based on reactive processes *and* the financial and sales models that are required to make these services profitable, *they are in direct conflict with everything project management.*

A project is

"A temporary endeavor undertaken to create a unique product, service, or result." —PMBOK® Guide 4th Ed., PMI.

"A temporary organisation that is created for the purpose of delivering one or more business products according to an agreed Business Case." —PRINCE2 Guide 2009 Ed., OGC

Literally, it is the opposite of all things day-to-day—the opposite of ongoing management.

When a senior sales representative or manager of an outsourcing company is forced or tries to provide a level of managed service more efficiently, he or she cannot use the same tools or adopt the same approach to do the same to project services.

A project's cost cannot be reduced; its price cannot be arbitrarily cut without impacting its delivery in some core, high-risk way. There is no next quarter or next financial year in which to reclaim losses made during previous service periods per project. It's a project, not an ongoing service. It has to be formed, deliver something, and then wink out of existence!

The reality of the pressures a management service outsourcing company has (from the focus and capability of resources, to the nature of work involved) means a managed service and a project management service are diametrically opposed in their focus, over-all management, and outputs. As customers, we cruelly smear the boundaries of these two conflicting service groups by expecting, indicating strongly, or outright demanding that our vendor reduce project costs when asking them to sharpen their pencil for other managed services or to align project services costs to the managed services cost model also provided. This has a compounding effect throughout the outsourcing relationship and levels of project services provided.

Whether it's a Telco, pure IT, or a hybrid provider, when providing a managed service, if the company also provides project services to the same company, the project services are minimized, bogged down, and hampered by "managed services" processes, approaches, and attitudes. The managed services "bias" slices through the effectiveness of project delivery and the flexibility that project management services require to be successful. They fill their projects with service staff, not project staff.

Many of these vendors' management do not understand or have little real experience in project management. Why should they? They're busy enough with managed service provision already. So sales guys draft figures that look good and populate staffing in bids with phantom staff with project roles that might as well be made up. They use arbitrary methodologies to create artifact lists and plans to make sales they will get a commission on. Senior management then takes random slices at project and project management costs because the lowered cost will be more palatable to us customers!

Customers and vendors need to be aware that if someone is cutting the price of a project, or if we are forcing the cost down on the project, something's missing from it. Project's cost what they cost, require the time and effort they require, and need to do the things they need to do. We can't make arbitrary budget cuts and expect the same results. Unless (an important note for executive managers of outsourcing companies) we also accept that our profit margin will be less, which if we truly accept this, this is a reasonable business decision. But then we should only hold our project services group to come in at the proportionate reduced profit!

A customer will still expect the vendor to deliver what they said it'd deliver, even if the profits are burned already by delivering something that was ill-conceived with...ah, bugger. This sounds familiar.

Also if we get vendors to sharpen their pencils around the resource rate level (the hourly or daily rate paritular resources will cost customers) then we should also expect to get what we pay for—that other peanuts analogy.

We should also understand that at some stage in the pencil-sharpening exercise there is a horizon that adversely effects quality and requires expensive rework to be done. Or more precisely, someone in a recovery role will get called in at some point when the project hasn't delivered what it meant to, is going off the rails, or has become hampered by a vendor's refusal to do further work and reset the project because it wasn't scoped or sized (including budget) properly in the first place.

The actual morals of this story are that IT projects cannot be treated as a "managed service." They are expensive, even when done well. We need to suck it up, accept it, and move on.

Supercaliflagellationexpialidocious— Or No One Likes a Smartarse

◇◇

OK, this is the last section of the "contributing factors" there are more, but I promised some self-flagellation in the introduction of this book so here goes. There is a point to it, and not because it just feels so good.

I guess I'm an OK IT PM; there are areas I'm really good at and some I need to spend a bit more attention on. I'm good at assessing things, shaping things, and sizing things accurately and early on. I'm pretty good at integrating things in IT programme and projects and man-aging and defining the complexities of priority, dependency, and sequence.

I am fantastically bad at maintaining interest once these things have been done. It takes an effort for me to manage something to com-pletion. I can and will do it and within cost, scope, time, and quality. But really, sometimes, yawn.

I can take a whole raft of project mess and the associated tangled sensitivities and vagaries and get it running again. I can determine that the best thing for it is to take the project out back and shoot it.

I can't always communicate "the vision" or expectations in a clear and concise way, and I can come across as an elitist know-it-all, which is not the way to inspire stakeholders to perform on a project.

And sometimes...just sometimes...I sit on some crucial decision or issue far too long than I should and I know I'm doing it!

At my worst, I guess, I'm arrogant, self-centered, egotistic, directive, task-orientated, and aggressive. I don't play well with others when I'm not getting my own way, and I have a very bad habit of not handling the navigation of social sensitivities within corporate structures; I end up feeling like a gothic nihilistic outsider with a will to power—not really the best person suited for project management.

But I can be reflective and take direction and advice. That's why there's a version twelve of this book. If I hold myself up to the light of my often stupidly high expectations, I have to admit that I can be found lacking in IT project management and that all those things that I'm not very good at, other people have already written books about, and not always project management books!

But that's why I have mentors and peers. I expect a good ear-bashing and arse-kicking from time to time if I need it.

Also, that kind of self-criticism and holding myself to the same flame as everyone else got me thinking, and I need to confess something to you.

In the midst of the chaos over the previous years as an IT PM, when running projects I often end up doing the same bad practice as everyone else. I don't get things documented. I write requests for change because my techs are too busy and then end up arguing at change management meetings instead of planning, monitoring, or controlling. I don't work to any particular methodology and end up completing the very list of "office administration" activities I listed previously, but without adherence to any project process or activities and their expected outputs.

I've realized that I go in all best-practice guns blazing. Over time, I make the same mistakes as everyone else, like not getting a signature on a contract because I get caught up in the horrific processes that are implemented and struggle to maintain what I know used to work in project management, and then I spend my time and personal energy constantly arguing with management about how to run projects properly.

Unfortunately, I have to admit that after a while, I usually just give up, finish off whatever I can do well, have a sulk, and move on...only this time around I decided to write a book about it.

What's more is how I got into project management in the first place. Are we ready for it? I was haloed in from a solutions architect role (or senior systems analyst back then), with absolutely no formal project management experience whatsoever—at least not enough to look after a $1M project.

But I remember thinking back then that I could do it. I'd run solutions from concept to implementation before and I could do projects. Wow, lucky I had an absolutely phenomenal consultant and professional project manager from the vendor who taught me a thing or two about how to manage his risk, my risk, the organisations risk, and the vendor's risk. He genuinely wanted me to succeed.

The rest of my transition to a professional PM reads as a story of good fortune.

Luck had it that in a subsequent position I got placed next to a professional PM who was a leader and active within PMI and PMINZ. He convinced me to become PMP certified and helped me through a "Oh my God, Dave, you didn't walk off the premises yelling, 'This is too hard, I quit,' as a contractor, did you?" kind of transition to professional project management. Yeah, there are some lessons learned there, and mostly around asking for help as a project manager before we pop.

But because of his ongoing mentoring and support, I got to work in a PMO based on the PMBOK® Guide and developed with the help of other professional project managers. The kind of environment where even if you discovered something that hailed very bad news (VBN), you were supported and the issues worked through.

Then because of all this support and work, I received some consultancy and review roles during a working sabbatical and even more mentoring and peer support from the consultancy's practice manager(s). You couldn't ask for better opportunities, peers, support, guidance, and mates. Then the earthquake struck...no I'm OK, it's just a little spec of sentiment in my eye.

Very Bad News (VBN)

Just thinking back to that VBN comment, I now always seem to be the harbinger of VBN.

When researching this book, it became clear that because of the general poor practice in IT project management, professional PMs spend inordinate amounts of time coping with its impacts and not really practicing "real" project management—more like constant project triage—and subsequently giving VBN from what we've discovered.

Even when hired to just run projects as opposed to review and recover them, we protect our interests and the interests of our clients by adopting a forensic and analytical approach to project management because so many of the basic practices aren't in place. Then we spend time building additional "mitigating" structures and processes for the gaps, try to reestablish compensating basic practice, and generally fall out with those staff insisting on keeping their poor practice. Finally, we enter into the strong discussions with the management that hired us.

This is an inefficient way of running projects and is not technically project management (yet another reason I have to include myself in the self-flagellating practice assessments); giving VBN immediately places professional PMs in a poor position of constantly having to become the agents of the angel of death. They always have to delve into the shadows to see what evil lurks there, holding private sessions with our peers and mentors to make sure the news is as bad as we think it is, battling project evils and injustices, and ultimately and inevitably becoming the harbingers of VBN.

Let's face it—this book is like sixty thousand words of VBN!

Holistically senior ITPMs, to manage everyone's risk, and at the risk of being labeled as doom and gloom merchants (again), have to actually step into the shadows to see what's there, and from the shadows, pronounce—objectively—what it is they see. This doesn't make them bad people.

But in this sense, there is a right and wrong way of doing things in project management and in IT despite the watered down recommendations and strong suggestions from the various professional groups that support project management. As a result of no one having the tenacity to say "do it this way or fail" what we now constantly find in the shadows is very poor practice (VPP). The truths about project professional approaches are written...they're black and white, yet everyone is so scared of prescribing how to do things in project management at the risk of offending someone or restricting a project manager's style (Please!), that massive gaps are opening up in the quality of its practice.

But this agent of the angel of death aspect is only part of the job; it shouldn't be the job itself!

One Last Nail

And for a final round of self-flagellation to finish this section off, this is all what I came up with when I realized that the only things those first few versions of this book would get me is labeled a crank, with people not listening to what I (and others) have been discovering in the shadows.

I have to include myself in the absolute mess which is IT project management, and admit that there's nothing special about me or what I do as a project manager—as much as my ego would choose to differ—and I just love that agent of the angel of death analogy. Cue fanfare of the dammed!

The only difference I can see is that I hold a raft of analytical skills around defining and resolving problem spaces, which ironically I learnt during my exposure to university computer science and information systems theory; and that each project is in fact an instance of a complex problem space requiring a solution.

I realized that I had been and am still actively employing these skills in my own practice of IT project management, basic fundamental analytical skills which allow me to build complex mental abstractions and then (try to) express them in words and pictures; and drive them to reality. That it's this coupling of IT analytical skills and experience, and professional project practices, which bring together for me a "practice" which enables me to perform better at managing IT projects, fix broken ones, and make "magic" predictions like some seer from Merlin's time—In exactly five weeks' time, when the moon is waxing, this project will be over budget and will only have completed half of its planned tasks for the period.

There is no magic here, just plain old simple (low level abstract) analytical processes and accepted project management practices; employed by an aging, jaded, cynical bastard, cursed with the plague of pragmatism.

Bah humbug! Bah humbug I say!

This is a good point in the book to get into the practices, approaches, and ways of looking at things that work for me as a project manager managing IT projects before that nervous twitch comes back.

3. PRACTICE MAKES PERFECT

Nun liebe Kinder gebt fein Acht
ich bin die Stimme aus dem Kissen
ich hab euch etwas mitgebracht
hab es aus meiner Brust gerissen
Rammstein: Mein Herz Brent

In this section there is commentary on the constitution of good practice in relation to the problems outlined previous sections. Starting with the application of good practice, the section continues to look at projects via analogies and from different angles, in attempt to describe good project management practice from new perspectives. Specifically this section covers the basic relational nature and structure of a project, the dynamism of a project and where a project manger should be seated within this dynamism, the adoption of an approach utilizing the wisdom of Sun Tzu, an example analogy of good project management practice on the battlefield, and the use and practice of methods of abstraction regarding project management, scope definition, and parallels to IT practices of abstraction. The section ends with a description of projects and associated practices and practitioners in the context of the international project management standard, frameworks, and methodologies in

order to dispel some myths around these standards and provide a concise commentary on how these standards relate.

As I've mentioned before, there's absolutely no point now, having laid out the problems I see, in describing what project management is and how to do it. This is because there are hundreds of books and other resources on the market already with this type of content and they seem to be making not a blind bit of difference?! (I had an exclamation mark at the end of this sentence, but really this is a good question in itself: why are these books and courses not making a difference? So I've added a question mark and an exclamation mark to emphasize this point.)

What I have done instead in this section is describe some different ways of looking at projects and comment on techniques and management practices I think are nonnegotiable, if we want our IT projects to succeed. Because of the sheer amount of practice material in the market and the fact that it's obviously not being applied, this can be the first item on how to improve the success rate of IT projects. Apply accepted practice.

Application of Practice

The application of basic practice should not be an individual thing and is simply not happening in the IT project management space.

It should not be left up to a project manager to decide what is right either. I've already described the habit that has occurred in the PRINCE2INO world because of this. No one is actually using PRINCE2. With the "respect the project manager" attitude has come the assumption that a project manager knows how to run a project! It's blatantly obvious that project managers in this category do not know how to run a project.

So this nonindividual approach to practice also means that a PM's boss must also know what is right in terms of basic practice to be able to assess whether good PM practice is being used and how it should be applied; this flows onwards and upwards. The project delivery or programme manager's boss must also understand the nature of projects at their level, and so on and so forth up to the portfolio level and strategic investment, up to the CEO.

This is what project management as a core corporate competency means. All roles within this particular virtual structure associated with project management must understand, at their level, the nature of projects and the techniques and methodologies associated with successfully managing them.

This is the next point to ensuring success in IT projects. We must stop hiring people into the IT project management space who have no skills, experience, or background in IT or project management. If we are hiring people from other sectors, industries, branches of the business, these new entrants must be put on a remedial programme that educates them in the nature of IT projects—no matter what their level within the organisation or expertise in other areas. This includes executive management and above who are new to project management concepts.

Several times I have been faced with project managers who have come in (off the street) from another profession because they thought they'd give IT and project management a go, sat their PRINCE2 certification, and were hired as project managers in the IT space. When it came to work on decent sized projects (as opposed to smaller projects that were treated as work requests in which the office administrator approach can work more effectively and is more cost effective than placing the overhead of total project management over the initiatives), they could not plan, forecast, or run a budget. These PMs had no idea what the shape of the projects they were working on should look like in terms of the technology being implemented. But because their bosses had no experience in project management either, they could not identify that just because they needed these project managers to be project managers, it didn't make them able to manage the projects to which they'd been assigned.

While I could mention that of course this "walk in off the street" wouldn't happen in PMI— just to be considered as a candidate to sit the exam, a person would either need a university degree and five thousand hours of project management experience or seventy-five hundred hours of project management experience— because of the sick coupling of PRINCE2 to IT that seems to be occurring blindly, this isn't really a good point and is more appropriate for other industries, which is also why there is a real need for many aspects of the PMBOK® Guide to be applied to IT projects—even PRINCE2 IT projects.

But it is simple. Want to ensure better success for IT projects? Then these first two points are simply nonnegotiable: make an effort to apply basic accepted practice and stop hiring inexperienced people in project management related roles throughout the levels of an organisation. Project management is complex enough to have its own landscape of formal tools and approaches, so it's time to start treating it as a profession, not a job.

Projects as Fractals

OK, you've been running around long enough; smashing the new project toys we got you and generally being a pain all afternoon.

No, you've been very, very naughty, so I am taking these toys until you settle down and become reasonable again.

Stop crying. No, you can't have PMBOK or PRINCE2. You can have the building blocks instead and be happy with that!

Basic Project Building Blocks

First let me express the premise of this section, which was first explained to me by a friend on their PMP preparation course. The fundamental aspect of project management is built of little building blocks. You know, like the ones we use to play with when we were kids; they were pretty colours and had letters or pictures on them. They were perfect little cubes that were limited only by our imagination.

Also, not only is project management built from building blocks, but if we put enough of these blocks together, they look like one huge a bigger block. Subsequently, if we put several of these blocks together, they look like a project—a really big block. But every project is different and so has different larger building blocks.

Don't believe me?

Well, once upon a time a man called Deming came up with a better way of getting things done and making things better as we went. More precisely, he produced a self-improving algorhythm for problem solving and implementing solutions. This was called the plan-do-check-act (PDCA) cycle of quality management. There is a huge amount of material about this cycle on the Internet I won't go into detail about here. (But note: if you don't know what this is, look it up online now.) This cycle basically meant that if we follow its basic steps in any activity and if we run through the process multiple times, then 1) the process itself will improve and 2) the outcome or solution will more likely be successful.

Now here's the deal: the plan-do-check-act cycle is the singular building block of everything project management in IT. This isn't new. SCRUM and SCRUM cycles are built on this premise, as is the PMBOK® Guide's common project management process interactions and the monitoring and controlling process group's interaction with all other project processes; it results in something called iteration.

The overarching structure within the PMBOK® Guide's process group model is made up of varying levels and magnitudes of the PDCA cycles, and even the PMBOK Guide's and PRINCE2's basic process structure lends themselves to adopting PDCA cycles as we travel from input through to outputs. This is no accident; the PDCA cycle isn't just some management methodology, it's a proven algorhythm for doing anything in life, improving how we do it along the way, and getting better results for our efforts.

Do It PDCA Style

At a fundamental level as an IT project manager, if we're not doing one of the actions in the cycle in any given minute of our day, we're doing something wrong.

It could be in communications, managing scope, reviewing finances, or drawing up a contract. Every higher-level action, process, or activity should be built on this basic cycle of actions. Whether it's any of the PRINCE2 processes and activities or the PMBOK Guide's process groups and project management processes, every one of them should have multiple iterations of the plan-do-check-act cycle applied to them as required.

Let's take an example such as the PMBOK® Guide initiating process group and PRINCE initiating a project process. As a phase or group or whatever, we should at least be planning on how to do the initiation. Undertake the initiation and check that it's been done satisfactorily, and then either move to the next phase or go back and plan-do-check-act through the initiation phase again, correcting those things we did during the initiation that didn't work the first time or killing the project in its tracks right then and there if it looks bad!

The same goes for planning; we need to plan the planning exercise first and then do it. We then check if the plans are appropriate and feasible, and then act by either redoing a round of planning or move onto the next phase.

Both PRINCE2's managing by stage and managing by exception principles and associated themes and processes consist of plan-do-check-act cycle architecture.

Projects, Iterations, and Overlaps

Here's where it starts to get tricky and I see most project managers fall. PDCA cycles aside, some project processes or phase focuses may have to be done over and over again until the results are good; and these repeated processes may have a different focus to the general or overall process we're completing, like doing our project planning phase process again in the middle of running or executing the project—or constantly as changes around our project affect it.

"Oh no, but we did planning already? We can only do it once!" I hear you say.

No, no, no, no, no! Projects aren't ever fixed and known until the very end when no one is working on them anymore, especially IT projects. Unlike the constraints that most IT PMOs place on their PMs, all that PRINCE2 and the PMBOK® Guide ever said—to paraphrase the two approaches completely and to make it perfectly clear.

"Oye snotface, here's a structure for the management of a project that generally occurs for all projects...you might want to follow it, or not, but it's worked for us. It might be different for your specific projects, so you might want to check if all our stuff is appropriate for each of your projects, and whatever you do, don't employ our stuff wholesale without checking that it suits your projects first and then tailoring it to the project's specific needs."

In other words, we may need fifty rounds of planning, or—if our present IT projects are any indicator—have to go back and complete earlier technical stages again and complete the associated project processes until we get the thing right. We may (and it's highly likely that we will) have to start an IT project again, midway through its delivery. Because each project will be different, whatever we do, don't just *blindly apply the project frameworks and methods, wholesale, to our projects*!

Yes, in an ideal world we'd start at the left hand side of the PMBOK® Guide and PRINCE2's project diagrams and gently and gracefully move right. But it's not an ideal world so we will never, ever, do this with an IT project. While the Change in IT section outlines many of the reasons why this will never happen (along with the rest of the book for that matter), what I want to focus on here is the project itself.

To boil it down even further at its most basic structure a project has a start, middle, and an end. No matter how many stages or phases our PMO has, the project methodology we've adopted or technology constraints force us to have, the project itself has a start, middle, and an end. Say it with me: every project has a start, middle, and an end. It looks like this:

There are also common things that happen for each part of a project.

When we begin a project, generally speaking we do a good deal of planning, forecasting, and defining whether its resources, scope, time, or hard cash. Generally speaking, we're setting the project up and making sure it will go well. The middle of the project is where we do the stuff we set out to do and make sure stuff is happening. At the end of a project is generally where we stop doing things and make sure things have been done.

Each part has a different focus but we'll also note that in each part of a project we are making sure how things are going, whether things have been done, and what things still need to be done and applying action to correct things that aren't looking that great. It's such an important aspect of things within a project that we should probably make the basic project look like this

Even at this point of definition we can see that there are many PDCA parallels with an overall project. But things are never that easy.

Because of a plethora of reasons, many of which caused me to write this book, projects are a little more complex than the basic model above.

In fact, if we look closely at each main part, then we would see that each part of a project has a start, middle, and an end. Like this

Start			Middle			End		
Start	Middle	End	Start	Middle	End	Start	Middle	End
Check Things								

Each of these starts, middles, and ends have their own special brand and focus of making sure we do things right and modifying things if they aren't right. Like this

Start			Middle			End		
Start	Middle	End	Start	Middle	End	Start	Middle	End
Check Things			Check Things			Check Things		
Check Things								

But even more confusing and very common is that many of these things may occur at the same time and are commonly referred to in PM speak as "overlap." Like this

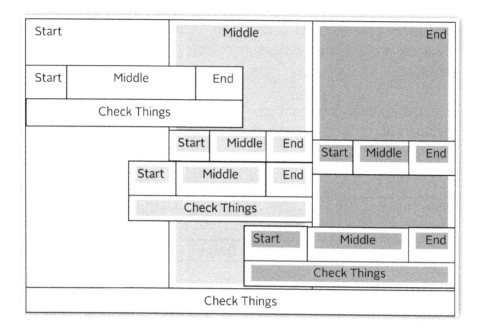

This is the reality in projects that generates confusion in IT projects. This is why the PMBOK® Guide isn't prescriptive per say and why PRINCE2 differentiates between "management stages" and "technical stages."

Also, these parts and things in most project approaches are called "processes" and they are the higher level building blocks of the project approaches found in PRINCE2 and the PMBOK® Guide.

Project Structures and Relationships to PDCA Cycles

Now, being mindful of the project definition above and the statement I made about the importance of PDCA cycles, if we then place the plan-do-check-act cycle across every possible process and activity in a project, we get planning when we're executing, checking when we're planning, and doing while we're closing. Whether we agree with my original building block statement or not, much of the noise and confusion in IT project management is caused by this confusing mishmash of activities, actions, and processes, with differing focuses and outcomes, which need to be occurring at the same time.

Its little wonder that all of this makes even understanding project management in IT extraordinarily hard, because in the context of this section:

- PDCA and project (process) definitions:
    - o Seem to contradict each other—planning while doing
    - o Can be confusing—planning the planning
- Project parts need to be done multiple times at different points in a project while completing PDCA cycles in every activity
- The accepted, grosser parts of a project and its activities may overlap and hence different flavors of PDCA actions overlap frequently, based on the project activities occurring concurrently.

It's even harder to actually apply appropriate project management practices in this environment, and even for those project managers with the right background and qualifications, it becomes easier just to go with the flow of day-to-day activities—especially so when their organisation has no idea about any of this.

However, the adoption of a PDCA approach to undertaking project management tasks and activities builds a discipline that is required for project management in IT projects. It's a discipline that mimics and matches the very nature of how projects are run successfully, so is inherently suited as a discipline of behavior for project managers.

It is in the fundamental nature of a project to be chaotic and go off track; it is fundamentally inherent within the PDCA approach to neutralize this particular project behavior. At the very least it will make us stop and think about what we are doing, why we are doing it, and how to do it better.

A Slight Pause for Elegance

It's time for a poetic reprise.

Think of it this way: Think of a tree. Think of the branching structure of that tree, right down to the ribs across the lamina of the leaves. This is the same pattern no matter what part of a tree it is grown. The tree is a fractal (a curve or geometric figure, each part of which has the same statistical character as the whole).

Now think of an IT project. Think of the cycle structure of that project, right down to the minute-by-minute cycles of that project. This is the same repeating pattern no matter what part or level of the project it occurs.

The IT project is a PDCA fractal—or should be.

Techniques To Manage the Madness

There are several important techniques that enable to manage the confusing cyclinc madness described above:

- Don't confuse everyday activities with project processes and activities. Get a better understanding of the processes, and then implement them where you can. Remember that project processes and activities result in project collateral or out-comes that fundamentally and measurably move the project forward.
- Be mindful of and put effort into identifying what activities are or should be happening in a project at any given time, phase, or stage, and what project process they relate to, what the outcomes of the process are, and how they relate to the next step in the project (i.e., what are the outputs going to be used for).

- Be mindful of and put effort into identifying what actions of the PDCA cycle are or should be occurring or need to occur
- Practice the PDCA cycle across every project process and activity: when you're gonna do something: plan it first (even if this is in your head), do it, check that it got the result you wanted (even if this is done in your head), then act to improve it if it needs it (yes—we too might just have to change what we're doing, how we're doing it, our behavior, our approaches to things or interactionse with people and stakeholders).
- Be mindful of and understand what's happening in IT project management and the project managers we're dealing with— they're most likely little more than office administrators

Projects As Vacuum Cleaners

Yeah, I know it's tempting to simply say projects suck (ah, thank you), but that's not what this section is about. This section builds from the last one on the cyclic nature of projects and tries to add momentum and animation to those cycles.

OK, here's the deal. Imagine the entire project cycle, the biggest one—we would define as "a project" —as a vacuum cleaner, picturing either the high level PRINCE2 process chart or the PMBOK Guide project management project groups diagram will do for this.

Add to these diagrams, on the right hand side, a funneled intake that sucks in everything in its path. If the project is healthy then the scoop primarily sucks in resources for processing in the body. At the back of this mental picture, instead of a bag to capture dust like a normal vacuum cleaner, we have another tube which spits things out in nicely defined chunks. Think of the tube spitting out those compacted cubes of trash metal that a car wrecking processing plant produces. If a project is healthy, this tube spits out deliverables or products depending on our particular project management camp definition, but they are the same thing.

OK, now we have our basic project vacuum cleaner and while the analogy is kind of humorous, the premise behind it is not. This model of a project—taking in resource from one end, processing the resource and producing something new we call deliverables or products at the other end— is another fundamental reality of all projects. It's what they do. It's their purpose. Every project since the beginning of time operates in this way no matter what methodology, framework, or approach. All projects have this dynamic structure of controlled change at the highest level producing things and stuff. The dynamism of the model is not complete and it's why I've built my model on a vacuum cleaner.

The model is not static, like a vacuum cleaner it moves through the space of our home, projects move through time, sucking in resources, issues, risks, and producing things by completing the processes within the project machine. So our mental model needs another component, a horizontal plane underneath it labeled time (in other words a straight line) that completes the model. Suffice to say that while the vacuum cleaner's purpose is to clean, the project's purpose is to produce deliverables or products, just to be clear in case any PMs reading this thought that they have to take a vacuum cleaner to work or that their project was to do the vacuuming.

Now let's switch on our model on and see what happens!

"Turning on" the project starts at initiation when the "instructions" on what the project is meant to do are loaded into the machine as scope definition (of some description). Like a vacuum cleaner is powered by electricity, a project is powered by cash in the form of budget and once switched on, a project is burning cash and consuming resource *and* gains momentum. However, if the wrong instructions are fed into this particular vacuum cleaner, it will never suck in the right resources or spit out the right products and deliverables.

The project manager is obviously the cleaner in this sense, although the thing about this project vacuum cleaner is that once moving, the project manager does not have to push it; it has its own momentum and the role of the project manager in terms of momentum is to control the speed of the little project beastie, which metaphorically has just gained its own life.

In fact, the PM has a crucial role because if they're not paying attention to what's coming up in the future, then the project will suck in all sorts of things, whether it's part of the project or good for its health, or not. The more things the project sucks in which aren't controlled—like scope and issues, the greater the momentum of the project will be, and the more out of control it will become, until its own kinetic energy sees it veering wildly of course, out of control, with a red faced PM running behind it, trying to catch up and bring it back under their control.

Also unlike a vacuum cleaner a project will not stop when the power (budget) is switched off. Our project vacuum cleaner runs on cash that includes negative budget too, and those resources and vendors have to be paid, regardless of whether or not there's any budget left! The thing about the project vacuum cleaner is that once it's started it takes more than the PM to stop it and all sorts of people have to agree to turn the vacuum off before it stops running (burning money), whether the PM wants it to or not.

OK, I think we have the model working for us, enough to apply the next point.

The Point of Focus for a Project Manager

What I see in IT project managment almost every day is that most if not all of us are either focused on the back end of vacuum cleaner, or the vacuum cleaner itself, or not even aware that we are managing something with this kind of model. To switch metaphors, everyone is behind the eight ball, or looking at it with a worried expression, waiting for it to explode.

Get this. Once running, our project vacuum cleaner will suck in everything—and I mean everything. It will suck in issues quicker than we can handle them. It will suck in environmental changes around it because that's what it does by nature. Its entire reason for being is to eat its way through resource and time to transform things, fueled by cash!

We seem to spend all of our time in day-to-day activities, thinking (hoping?) that it's project management, and continually whining, in a dazed and confused manner, about the problems our project is having. We whine about the fact that our technical change was canned at the last minute and about the fact that a resource was taken off the project without anyone telling us that someone is—yet again—being mean and unreasonable. To be frank, accepted professional project management practice would have it that the associated messes are entirely our fault as the PM.

It's a PM's role to avoid or manage issues before they happen, or at least identify them early. That's right! We can do that!

If there is no one watching where the project is headed, the project will fail!

As a PM, it is not our job to arrange things day-to-day so that other things get done (and by day-to-day I don't mean in the PRINCE2 context of Stage management, but doing things outside of the context of project processes and activities). It's not to make that phone call, chase up that resource or manager, run that report; we seem to do anything but project management! PRINCE2 PMs seem to do anything but project management.

That's not a criticism of PRINCE2, far from it. As discussed above, it's a criticism of people calling themselves project managers, programme managers, and PMO managers who have the PRINCE2 certifications but have no idea what project management is at a detailed level or how to do it. It's not acceptable to think or assume our project executives have the time, skills, or experience to undertake this focus; this is what the PM is for.

In PMI practice we are taught two basic premises, or key principles of project management, to avoid bad things from happening.

1. Continually look ahead of the project: a day, a week, a month, two months, a year
2. Replan and resteer the project iteratively and continually given the findings of 1) above while doing 1) above

PRINCE2 supports this even though it doesn't specifically state it; that's why there are management stages.

Basically (and assuming we were attending a good PMP course and not some accelerated "all the tricks we need to pass" course, which are prevalent out there), if we did not understand the simple double-premise above, we were taken out back and beaten until we understood how important it was.

In PRINCE2 this is not emphasized because it is inherent within the PRINCE2 principles and themes and embedded within PRINCE2's managing processes and focus of the PM completing day-today activities, this has obviously been misunderstood as doing admin tasks. Here's the problem: PRINCE2 is an awesome methodology, but PRINCE2 *only works if our project managers or project executives in some inastances know how to manage projects and have the proven techniques to do so.* Unfortunately, PRINCE2 does not focus on techniques that need to be applied in project management for projects to be a success. PRINCE2 respectfully assumes the project manager can take care of this stuff. It tells the PM when to do things, and at a conceptual level what to do also, and puts in place managed boundaries and delegations to ensure that checking and issue and tolerance escalation is performed, which is perfect. It does not explain how to do the things we are meant to do. The PMBOK® Guide does.

For example, in PRINCE2, variances in accepted or approved tolerances are escalated as soon as the tolerance in question is *forecast* to run over or under its tolerance. This will only work if the PM in question knows what a forecast is, what it's for, and how to do it accurately. This is one of the definitive arguments for adopting multiple project toolsets. Like PRINCE2 and the PMBOK® Guide, again, they aren't mutually exclusive.

The majority of issues we experience in IT project management can be avoided! Those that can't be avoided can be seen from a mile off if only we know how to look, and at least we could tell our stakeholders about them coming. When we know how to use the techniques we can to pretty much see into the future with a great deal of confidence!

This is another basic premise of project management that PMI and the PMBOK® Guide provides but that PRINCE2 does not emphasize, setting expectations with stakeholders as early as possible about all things to do with the project. This will remove the majority of bad behaviors, arguments, and backstabbing by making everything transparent (another PMI premise) and clear—so that no one is in the dark about what is happening—so can't feign ignorance as an arse-covering technique later on.

But how can we set expectations about things yet to happen if we are not looking ahead and planning accordingly, in other words if we cannot see them?

Looking Ahead

Getting back to the project vacuum cleaner, the project manager's job is not just making sure the vacuum cleaner is running properly and producing what it's meant to; it's also actually to look at what's coming up in the project's landscape and steer the project away from obstacles, problems, and issues before the project gets there.

The tasks for day-to-day project management do in fact involve phone calls and administrative duties, fair enough, but not without context of the project process, activity, and associated PDCA cycle presently occurring or at the expense of basic project management practices, which have to be taught.

Techniques To Manage the Madness

There are several important techniques to come out of this.

- Go and learn some good how to tools. Again, there's no point me writing this stuff in this book when there's already good reference material out there (just not the understanding that needs to go with it about why it's so important).
- Add looking ahead to your daily and weekly tasks to try and find issues and problems before they occur. What's happening next week, next month, next year and how is it relevant to our project?
- Plan and steer the project iteratively and continually. Now that we're looking ahead, what can we do about the things that may go wrong? If we have an important technical change coming up in two weeks, what can we and our project teams feasibly do today to make sure it gets approved and is executed successfully?
- Don't stop there. Set expectations based on what we've found out and what we propose to do about it, with the relevant project stakeholders. Note that they will probably not understand how we can see the issues and impacts coming up, so we will have to explain the process we went through to see it.

Projects as Battlegrounds

In this section I outline yet another way of looking at projects and note that the most important word in this section will be the word "sometimes."

Sometimes it pays to treat a project and the environment it exists within as a battleground, and related programme as the campaign season. To take our approach to the project as the general in charge of the army that will fight the campaign's battles.

I've said before that a project is an agent of change. Because of this a project will "kill" everything in its path that needs changing, literally laying waste to the status quo and creating in its wake the new state. Further, environments that we execute projects in are often hostile—maybe not to begin with, or overtly, but definitely by the time we make change occur.

As such, approaching a project from a "military" standpoint can sometimes be a better way of holding one's position within a project. For example, the project manager protects his or herself and team or organisation to ensure better success and to provide great insight into the project's true chance of success.

Sun Tzu

As clichéd or hackneyed as it may seem, the military wisdom of Sun Tzu may also be applied to IT project management. If we are a senior PM undertaking very complex IT projects, and especially if we are a contractor, I strongly recommend you add *The Art of War* to your project management library.

Here are some examples of this analogy that I've used in the past.

It is important to understand the status and ability of the courts in question. Is our court in order? Are the managers and executives related to the project fighting, bickering and quarrelling? Are there power plays occurring that will affect the project? Is there an alignment and agreement of vision regarding the coming campaign season in which our project will occur? Do we think assassinations will occur during our project? If so will the incoming sponsor or project executive or pro-gramme manager or change in management whip the raison d'être out from under our feet, leaving us high and dry holding the project baby? Are we or is the project an agent of a disgruntled faction of the court? Or does the project represent the court's intentions and interests?

What about in other courts? The courts of the vendors, the cus-tomer, what state are they in? Are they receptive, capable, and pre-pared for the coming campaign?

And as for the project itself, is the team prepared? Have the logistics of the project truly been worked out? In terms of risks and issues, is the project truly resourced enough to complete its overall mis-sion? What if each major issue is a battle in itself, can the project resources take the strain for the entire campaign?

Where is the project heading in terms of its implementation foot-print on the business and real human beings? This is the landscape of the battlefield; do we have the right resources to fight on this field? Or will diplomacy win over mite?

The project parallels to *The Art of War* are almost endless and extraordinarily valuable. Even if we never actually materially change anything about our projects because of viewing a project this way, I can guarantee that we will gain insight into our project to a level never experienced before.

Battle of Gaugamela or Arbela[6]

I'm sorry the military analogy is not over yet; here's a military parallel regarding good practice.

In 331 BC, Alexander the Great led a decisive victory against the Persians and their great king Darius III. He did so by using highly trained, drilled, and experienced, soldiers, and by taking advantage of the terrain of the battlefield by utilizing successful tactics the soldiers afforded him.

His crack army of forty-one thousand faced an army of upwards of eighty-seven thousand Persians of which only twenty thousand could have been considered good troops. The rest of the Persian army was considered to be made up of poorly trained and armed troops.

In terms of IT project management, Darius can be seen to have taken a "chuck mud at it until it sticks" approach, relying on a practice with no great depth or skill of application. He showed up and made a reasonable show of arranging his army, but relying on the sheer weight of his numerical superiority—complacently thinking that more and more resource would win the day.

Alexander on the other hand had a smaller army and all were seasoned in the appropriate tactics, armed with the tools required to be successful on that particular battlefield (in this instance, longer spears and the methods of using them).

Upon entering the battlefield, Alexander was already using his knowledge and experience (practice) to set his army up for success. During the battle he both utilized a particularly difficult maneuver with his main force because of their training and experience, which

---

6 Battles are commonly named after the town, village, settlement, etc they are closest to. In this instance the villages of Guaugamela and Arbela are almost equidistant from the actual site of the battle; hence the battle is known by both names.

enabled the army to deal a devastating blow to the opposing army, and also to remain flexible and enact a reactive defense when the rear of the army was threatened.

Meanwhile, and to paraphrase significantly, all that Darius could do was watch as the majority of his army crumbled before his eyes or fled the field of battle. So disordered had his troops become that he was neither able to utilize his good troops to any affect, or undertake tactics with them that would have ensured some success. In effect, like so many IT PMs, once the proverbial hit the fan, he was unable to regain control.

In the military analogy above Alexander used seasoned and skilled officers and soldiers in combination with the appropriate tools and tactics to win the battle. The IT project management equivalent here is that there is no substitute for skills and experience, and that when these are combined with good practice, project success is ensured.

Projects as Expressed Abstraction

We should not underestimate the extraordinary need for an IT project manager to have the ability to construct multidimensional abstractions when managing IT projects. By abstraction I mean the ability to shape visualizations of reality in our heads and map relationships between important parts of that abstraction.

This need for abstraction is then partnered with the just-as-important-needs for the project manager to express abstractions externally, communicate those expressions to others, and move through their own abstractions, updating and reevaluating them as information comes to hand or situations present themselves.

A good example of this is the Gantt chart. What is the humble Gantt chart if not a linear abstraction of tasks and their dependencies over time in chart form? Another good example is the hierarchical work or product breakdown structure, it is not the products, tasks and events themselves, but a representation of these things in diagrammatic form that the project needs to undertake or build.

The issue is (especially when completing a project review) I never seem to find any of these artifacts of abstraction in the project management collateral built by a project or its manager. There are often Gantt charts or schedules for Africa, but never any WBS or PBS collateral. By what method was the schedule formed? In fifteen years of IT and IT projects, I have never seen dependency charts (called a network diagram, but because IT has its own "network diagrams" I'll use the term dependency chart in this book to distinguish between the two and keep noting it) or precedence diagrams. For an industry that experiences so much change in any given project, a set of dependency charts are a critical artifact to produce, more important than a detailed schedule, but no one produces them.

For clarity, while from a behavioral perspective the basic building blocks of a project are the PDCA cycles, from a practical perspective in terms of ordering and sequencing the project's activities to produce its products and deliverables, the abstraction of scope in the form of project tasks, activities, events, product lists, and effort are the basic building blocks for the majority of tools used to represent a project.

But it's the one thing we fail to define using these tools over and over again.

Here are my "must haves" and views when it comes to the abstraction of project scope in the form of the tools we need to be using to express them—and subsequently gain the visibility needed to control an IT project.

Scope

Many projects I get handed are more than 200 percent over budget and late by months because the people that formed the project in the first place did not know how to size and shape the work involved to begin with.

As mentioned before, there is better material out there, scope management and time management of the PMBOK® Guide and PRINCE2's focus on a product regarding scope practices, but there are three things about the abstraction and definition of scope any project manager needs to know.

1. The definition of scope evolves over the life of a project, pro-gressively getting more detailed, until the abstract thing has been turned into a real thing (the final definition of scope) a product or deliverable.
2. The basic sequence for the evolution of scope definition is to start at a high level with a single statement that captures everything that needs to be done or built, then progressively

detail the scope iteratively as we investigate the how, what, who, how much and why of getting this high level "thing" done.

3. As the project progresses, scope definition is and must be translated via abstraction into tools used to manage different aspects of the project, and those tools maintained; because if scope in a project changes, so does every other aspect of project management.

The application of the items above is a core project management skill.

If project managers are not completing and maintaining scope definition, project management is not being done. Our IT projects will fail.

Defining Requirements & Scope

It's not surprising that we have to do both of these well, and in progressively more detail. Defining both requirements and scope before we get too far down the track and then randomly and arbitrarily agree the size of something and do it! But it just doesn't happen. It's one thing to be asked to do something even at a high to midlevel of detail—please upgrade ABC system from x.y.z.1 to x.y.z.6, please move us from Lotus Notes to Microsoft Infrastructure. But this won't get us a project that we can control and get done on time and budget to a given level of quality.

Even an RFP response does not provide a basis from which to plan a project in detail. Scope definition has to be worked on collaboratively with all parties, and agreed! A project's scope definition is more than a set of requirements. But day-after-day we jump right into business case, project initiation and/or contract formation, with scope left at a grouping of loose, vague, but nevertheless binding statements. Then we expect technical resource to do their jobs and produce it for us, only to find out that midway through the work that there's actually a specific piece of prerequisite work to be done within the scope of one of these statements, which has just blown our time out by weeks and added more effort to our project than we started with.

This is a short section compared to other books on the subject because other people have spent a good deal of their time explaining how to define scope and requirements better than I can, but here's an important summary on requirements and scope definition.

This is Wrong!

Don't jump from some vaguely defined idea or request and into forming scope by drawing up statements of work or similar contracts, and then start the work. This is a significant reason as to why we have to hire recovery PMs to fix our projects. This right here. Nothing else. Just this basic mistake of diving into the work before it has been properly defined and formed.

THIS IS RIGHT!

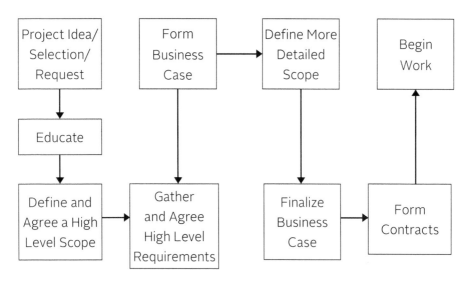

Educate means just that. Start telling vendors and customers alike that they can save money, headaches, and stress later on by doing these basic steps first.

Requirements gathering is a collaborative effort and so is scope definition! But it's high level at this stage and should be defined enough to complete the other initiation steps and agree on a delivery methodology or approach.

Begin work means shape the project so that it will be in a fit shape to execute *and* translate the scope further—in other words, translate the scope that's been handed to us at this stage into something we are confident and comfortable with handling (executing).

Hey, if things look too complex when we start or everything is too vague to make the gamble to do a project, how about forming scoping or exploratory projects first? Or properly adopting PRINCE2 and its initiation stage boundary? Or how about iterating through this entire sequence in a more agile way by taking a slice of the top initiative priorities and applying this entire treatment to them first?

Remember someone has to pay for these activities!

We will save money in the long run by paying for these activities up front; otherwise they will occur in an ad hoc, fragmented and retrospective fashion, while the project is running and busy trying to actually build things! And never be really, truly, properly done and cost so much more to complete!

Requirements Are...

Requirements are statements that detail what is required by that upgrade, development, implementation, or shift of infrastructure. They are a list of what a human being needs the automated system in question to do (functional requirements or user stories), a list of the bounds of how the system and its infrastructure will have to run to support those functional requirements (nonfunctional requirements), and any "work in the background" that is necessary to support both functional and nonfunctional requirements (technical debt).

As such, the relationship of requirements to scope is that they help shape what needs to be done and to what level of quality. Requirements are used at the beginning of a project to help constrain and form scope for execution, and during the project to assess when something has been done successfully.

Just to make it harder requirements can change during the project, hence the business justification for the associated scope of the project may change with them. When or if this happens we need to return to the beginning of the scope definition process to assess the impact of the changes to requirements (and hence scope) and hence the justification of spending money completing the scope.

Every IT project has requirements and needs them documented. Every IT project!

If there is rapid or constant change in requirements throughout the expected lifecycle of the project, *do not undertake a waterfall approach to scope and requirements*—or else, by the time you come to test if the requirements from the beginning of the project have been met, they will have changed and the product will not be fit for purpose for the present set of requirements.

This is what adopting a more agile approach is all about. It allows us to stay flexible with scope (in its broadest definition) and its execution by undertaking a smaller, well-defined scope at any one time.

The Business Case Is...

The business case is not only a mechanism to justify the expenditure to execute scope initially (i.e., do a project), it is a control mechanism that must be used throughout a project to ensure the justification for scope execution is maintained and that the associated initiative's objectives are being met by project delivery. It should be checked periodically throughout a project and especially when requirements and/or scope changes.

For instance, we may have permission to spend 1.5 million pounds on a project, but what if it will now cost 2.5M because a new piece of infrastructure, connectivity, functionality is required? Does the business case justify this amount of change?

Scope Is...

Scope is all of the products[7] that need to be built (including services), the activities that need to be completed to build those products, and any procurement of gear on which to build on that will meet specified requirements to enable the project to meet its objectives within the constraints of an approved business case (set of business reasoning).

Initially, these should be expressed as statements with varying levels of detail—given the requirements provided *and* purpose or audience of the statement being made—a summary scope statement or project product description for management to understand, or on which to base further detailing, is different to a detailed list of statements on which to base activity and task definitions (see below estimates).

Eventually, for every requirement, a scope statement similar to the following could and should (in most cases) be made: "If [the system] need[s] to do this, then we have to build/configure/do this."

---

7   From this point on the word "product" should be used interchangeably with deliverables—the reason for this is explained further on in the book

Scope definition is also a mapping of any dependencies between the products to be built and project events (more often than not) to be expressed diagrammatically so that activities (effort) and scheduling (time) can further be defined and sequenced. This is such an important aspect of scope definition and control for IT projects that I have included it below as a separate section on abstraction.

A Better Approach to Managing Scope?—A Focus on Products

There is a subtle but powerful difference between the PRINCE2 approach to defining scope and other more traditional methods. It's powerful in the context of this book because so many people that I ask—technical and project management orientated alike—cannot describe to me what a project's scope is to save themselves.

Everyone nods their heads knowingly when we say that scope is the "what" of the project world—in other words what the project will do and produce. Yet, one of the most common things I have to do when trying to fix projects is define or redefine the scope of what was meant to be done in the first place. More often than not it will be the first time in the project's history that the scope has been defined to a level where it can be assessed against the project's success criteria—if that's been defined—another thing I have to do frequently.

One of the main reasons for this is because the work breakdown structure (WBS) approach, which focuses particularly on activities and tasks that need to be completed to build a project's products in regards to the project's phases or stages, not the products themselves. Now there is nothing wrong with this approach if:

- Requirements and acceptance criteria have been specified clearly
- Project managers are professional (they understand and implement project management techniques) and are experienced in delivering successful projects

- The project management environment in which the project being completed, is mature with robust and sound processes

But with all this noise around project management in IT already and without knowing how to define scope using the accepted techniques, (blindly) only using the WBS approach for projects abstracts the management of things and stuff a project has to produce into further obscurity. This is especially so if the principal or only reason we're using work breakdown structures is because our financial or project management system directly supports a WBS.

PMOs that have adopted the WBS approach without due consideration often lose sight of the products their projects are meant to produce. These PMOs end up producing and managing scope processes that only cater for effort and time without the context of "what" was meant to be done in the first place (and as for assessing value for money—don't even go there).

While it may be good to utilize existing systems for the sake of efficiency and money saving, it is never good practice to adopt a project management approach without first considering the types of products and projects that approach has to support and the ability and experience of the PMs that will have to use the approach.

This is why I am suggesting that, outside of user stories and iterations of scope development, the PRINCE2 theme of focusing on products and its technique of defining products is the solution to this particular situation.

A thing or product is easy for everyone to understand and get their head around. It's more immediately intuitive than a deliverable. I mean what's a deliverable? Oh, it's a thing or product you say? Well why don't we just call it a product then? It's easier for everyone to understand.

Grouping all the tasks and activities under a product heading to capture all the things that need to be done to produce the product is far more immediately intuitive and comprehensive than listing all the activities and tasks under deliverable and phase headings that have been defined to manage and sectionalize a project—not a product.

Yes, I agree. This product approach (alone) won't work for all projects. Trying to manage systems integrations for wind farms relied on the dependency mapping, sequencing, and management of events as much if not more than the dependency mapping, sequencing, and management of the products or the deliverables we were trying to integrate. Yet again, here's an argument for using multiple project tool-sets like PRINCE2 and the PMBOK® Guide. Getting the message yet?

But for the sheer majority of projects I've had experience with, the product-focused approach would have been a complete approach to managing this aspect of scope definition that was clearer and more intuitive than the traditional "work breakdown" approach. And in the spirit of PRINCE2's tailoring emphasis, we could in fact use both as the project need dictated. Further that it can in fact be developed to couple or map with a more agile approach like SCRUM, involving user stories and the like.

Before anyone starts clamoring on about how PRINCE2 doesn't put any emphasis on gathering requirements, this was my first thought also, but I suggest we look closer at PRINCE2's approach to quality and controls, and the fact that without a clear definition of the quality acceptance criteria for a particular product, that product and the work package it is part of will not be authorised!

Inherently, without clear requirements, clear quality acceptance criteria cannot be formed in the product description. So if we were thoroughly implementing the PRINCE2 methodology, a project would never be able to start work on a product that did not have its products' requirements well defined.

The Evolution of Scope

Before moving on to other aspects of scope definition, it may pay to outline the general evolution of scope and the varying relationships to other areas of project management and its accepted management tools.

Generally, the evolution in the abstraction of scope occurs in greater detail until scope is defined enough to structure a project so that it can be executed, and then continually updated so that the project can be controlled as expected.

These are the common and accepted tools of professional project management. All are critical to ensure the success of a project, and if they are not in use, project management is not really taking place.

The Evolution of the Definition of Scope—or what a project needs to do

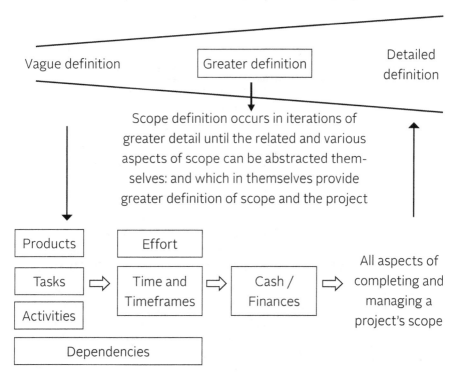

Evolution of Abstractions or Tools	Definition of or Relationship to Scope
Initial idea or request	First embryonic expression of a project's scope
(High Level) Scope Statement or Product Description (PRINCE2)	A bounded yet nondetailed expression of scope, with more clarity than the initial idea, and a (initial) delineation of what is accepted as "bounded within scope"—in other words what is accepted to be done and created by a project. An initial Product Description—literally an early summary of the main products to be delivered by a project—binds scope in the same way as a Scope Statement—setting out what will and won't be included in the main products of the project.
Requirements	A set of needs and wants which constrain and shape scope (the things to be done and produced to meet those needs and wants), and ultimately define a successful delivery of scope.
Detailed Scope Statements	A further round of statements describing what products are required in more detail.
Tasks & Activities	A listing of all the work required to build the products that are accepted within scope.
Estimates of Effort	An expression of the probable effort required to be completed against every task and activity, to build the products, which are accepted within scope.
Detailed Product Descriptions (PRINCE2)	A further round and decomposition of product definition to capture detail about what is required of every product node accepted within scope—including quality aspects of the products—See Quality Based Artifacts.
User Stories	A method of defining scope and quality expectations for products by writing a short story around needs the product or how it should behave, and how this will be viewed as successful.

Evolution of Abstractions or Tools	Definition of or Relationship to Scope
Business Case	A definition of the business reasoning to prove why a project and its scope should be undertaken in the first place, and an outline of the expected business benefits that will be gained by completing the project's scope.
PBS Product Breakdown Structure (PRINCE2)	A hierarchal expression of a component breakdown of all products to be provisioned within scope.
WBS Work Breakdown Structure	A hierarchal expression of a component breakdown of all tasks and activities that need to be completed to complete the creation of the products to be provisioned within scope.
Product Backlog	A list of business prioritized products or "product increments" typically used by SCRUM.
Timeframes	The modeling of the length of time it will take to complete the delivery of the project's products, using the tasks and activities required to deliver the products and the estimates of effort involved, and taking into account resources available to complete the tasks and activities.
Precedence Mapping/ Diagram and Dependency Chart (Network Diagram)	A mapping of the relationships between events, tasks and activities, and the delivery of products, to show precedence or the order in which things must be done to complete all of the products within scope. Precedence Diagrams also include elements of time estimations which can be used to derive a project's critical path—the key sequencing of scope delivery which will affect the entire project should something go wrong.
Product Flow Diagram (PRINCE2)	A mapping of the relationships between products and their delivery, to show precedence or the order in which the products within scope must be completed.

Evolution of Abstractions or Tools	Definition of or Relationship to Scope
Schedule and Gantt Chart	A mapping against time of tasks and activities, their sequencing and dependencies, needed to produce the products within scope.
Quality Based artifacts	A definition of the measurement and methods of review used to ensure that every product within the scope of a project is fit for purpose and meets requirements. In the PMBOK® Guide the quality artifacts are usually compiled within a separate Quality Management Plan; in PRINCE2 the components of quality are compiled against each Detailed Product Descriptions.
(Financial) Forecast	A modeled estimation of the money it will take to complete the production of all products within scope.
Contracts	A legal definition of a portion of the scope to be delivered by specific parities/ organisations.
Baseline	An agreed "snapshot" of all of the approved facets or aspects of delivering the scope of a project—used as a basis against which to track the progress and health of a project.
Progress Reports	A periodical or ad hoc summary definition of how well a project's scope is being delivered compared to an accepted baseline, sourced from the tools above (not made up or censored).

Those tools with PRINCE2 in brackets are specific to the PRINCE2 methodology. Although PRINCE2 mentions most of the other tools, it does not provide detail on how to use them, and makes assumptions but no recommendations that they should be used.

I am going to put my neck on the line here, ignore all that PC non-sense, and specify that until scope is being evolved in the manner described above, using all of the appropriate tools with project managers who understand how to wield them and the aspects of a project they relate to, IT projects will continue to fail. All IT project managers must be well versed in the techniques and tools of developing scope in this manner. It is not an option, should not be left to the PMs choice, and is definitively a huge contributing factor to why IT projects keep failing.

Estimates and Iterating Through Them

There are proven methods for estimation and a technique for building more confidence in them.

It should be noted that for the next few sections I outline definitions I use for estimating. These definitions seem to change, even between the PMBOK® Guide versions. These definitions are largely what I learned on my PMP course and modified by experience in different organisations

Producing Estimates—Order of Magnitude (OoM)

As a PM, we'll be asked to come up with estimates at all stages and phases of a project and should produce different estimates at different points in time of the life of a project. In other words, as more and more information comes to us throughout the project lifecycle about the size and shape of the project as its scope is defined and evolves, we will be able to produce more accurate estimates of how much a project will cost, until its finished *and our final estimate is based on how much it actually cost—plus or minus 0 percent!*

This is commonly called an order of magnitude approach and expressed by a number plus or minus a certain percentage. Again, there is a lot of information on the Internet about this. Please research before continuing if you are not familiar with this technique.

Note here that producing more than one estimate, with more accurate and narrow bounds, is using an order of magnitude and doing it iteratively over time. The following orders of magnitude are the most common ones I have to use in IT project management. Commonly, the actual number we come back with is called the point estimate, and the plus or minus percentages the range.

The Ballpark

How much will it cost, finger in the air, drawn up on the back of a napkin, short of pulling numbers out of somewhere best not mentioned?

If someone asks us for this then we should ensure they expect an answer of a figure plus or minus 100 to 200 percent or more, essentially meaningless but still an important first stake in the ground.

We probably haven't got much information or won't spend much time developing the estimate, but it is a fair question for our execs to ask. We should stop whining and find them an answer. And note that answer might be "I can't really say at this point in time, without spending a bit more time on it and talking to some senior technical resource. Give me two days to get back to you."

But have a go; you'll be surprised at what you can come up with even in an hour over a coffee with your best tech, and don't forget to provide the range of costs that will come back, as well as the point estimate.

The Working Figure

I've sat down with as many different resources as the nature of the project requires, I've applied at least *three to four out of the common estimating techniques* listed below, and I'm ready to provide a figure of plus or minus 25 percent.

That's it. It may be a bit higher or lower (up to 50 percent even) but it's the only figure I'm going to provide without going into detailed planning and/or technical discovery and requirements gathering.

That's right no detailed requirements have been gathered at this stage. This itself is considered bad practice by many, but its reality. So my estimates at this stage always go across to their audience with a strong caveat that goes like this:

"This estimate is due a variance of plus or minus 25 percent, however this figure may change during detailed planning and requirements gathering if information which was not visible at this level of estimation (and the work that went to producing it) comes to hand." (Feel free to use this statement or a modified version of it.)

Also this estimate goes across with areas of likely variance—yes, we need to do our homework here and set expectations of what could not possibly be seen in detail at this point in time. Note that these will be the areas our techs are worried about or vague about. Doing this now will open the way for good relations in the future and enable most variances found at a later date to be swallowed whole by sponsors because we set the expectation early that variance in these areas are likely to occur.

The Control & Baseline

We've completed another round of detailed planning by this stage, technical, requirements (hopefully) and project, following on from the working figure we provided earlier, enough for us to now call the point confidently.

So this is it. The only, smallest, variance we should work to—plus or minus 10 percent.

If people don't like this then I suggest that its perfectly acceptable not to stick around and, at the very least, that its quite understandable to be found at the pub that night sobbing in frustration to our peers—that yet again no one got to grips with basic estimating techniques and processes.

The reason for this percentage range is that a project or stage outturn envelope (the variance likely to occur between now and the end of a project or stage) in the sheer majority of cases can never be known better than plus or minus 10 percent until very near the end of those parts of the project *because of the rate and amount of change that is likely to occur before the project (or portion of it) is completed*. We are lucky the project management profession (and applied management and engineering sciences behind this area of knowledge) can even get this control estimate down to this level!

Also from this point of estimation onwards we need to be calling out anything that's added or taken away from the project's scope—now we have defined it. The situation we have today—in every other industry in the world—is called the project baseline.

If we add or take something away then this will change the baseline *and a new one should be created* based on the addition or subtraction of scope. We don't get to keep the original baseline and then hold the project to it when we are formally agreeing changes to what the project originally was meant to complete. We can, however, use the "original baseline" as a reference against what the project and its business objectives originally set out to accomplish.

Understand when we don't listen to reason before completing the right estimating processes (which is because of our egos or the fact that someone has called out arbitrary numbers or delivery dates to our exec team), we keep recovery project managers like me in work—yes!

And here's a real doozey. If we come in under budget more than our lower bound (-10 percent) in an uncontrolled manner (e.g., outside of agreed and managed change control and associated tolerances), then we have failed just as it would if we came in over budget. Why? Because it shows that our estimation or project initiation techniques and our controls were unsound and now no one can trust them going forward, and that we weren't really in control of the project to begin with.

Applying the Basic Estimation Techniques

As already mentioned as an IT PM fairly often we are asked to and need to complete project estimates.

Forgive the frankness, but as a project manager, estimating and forecasting goes with the territory. If we can't do it, then perhaps calling ourselves a project coordinator instead may give a more accurate view for the people hiring us. It is something expected of the junior project manager—albeit with review and assistance from their seniors—and definitely something an intermediate and senior project manager should be able to produce on their own.

Don't hate me for saying the above, because an error during these processes can and is costing our clients or customers millions of dollars and pounds. If we can't do these basic estimating tasks then the appropriate action is to let people know this, not hide the fact, fudge the results, and cause yet more project IT failures.

If we can't produce or understand estimates, then we can hardly track against them or understand the resulting baseline when managing the project. Hence we can hardly call ourselves project managers if we can't do this most fundamental of project management tasks.

Understand, even if we have little or no background in technical matters, that we don't have to come up with the estimates ourselves, although we should be experienced enough in IT to be able to understand and verify what a technical resource is telling us. If we can't, see the project coordinator comment above.

What we do have to do is guide the technical resources and management involved in the project through a set of processes that will complete fairly solid—giving the order of magnitude we are expected to achieve—estimates for the up-in-coming work.

On larger pieces of work, we will need to form a team to complete the estimations and we will have to be especially mindful of their dynamics and interactions, as the process is highly pressured by the need for accuracy and the kind of resources we will need can be highly emotive about their own opinions. Fortunately, there are common and proven techniques we can use as a PM to do estimation successfully.

There is a lot of material out there that covers these techniques in detail. The following sections provide guidelines and notes only on the most common and proven estimating techniques.

Using Expert Advice

Simply put, talking to resources with the experience, qualifications, and knowledge about the project we are sizing. They will have history, will have done it before, or will be able to use their experience in a similar area to help shape and verify things.

Note we have several uses for the experts.

- To shape estimates
- To verify assumptions and estimates that have been used during other techniques they have not been part of
- To verify our own treatment of the estimate once we have completed our job

Expert advice includes ourselves as PMs and other PMs/PgMs because although we are shaping up a technical/IT piece of work, the estimates have to include the "overhead" of running the project as a project, including our and our PMO's time!

Using Previous Projects

This approach is a series of questions that we go through to see if something that has been done before can be shaped to fit what we are trying to estimate at the moment. It goes like this: we ask ourselves these questions (and take experts along with us).

- Is there a project/undertaking that is similar to the one we're looking at doing?
- What is different about that project to this one (e.g., environmental differences, number of users/vendors)? What's been asked to be completed?
- Can we model either all or some parts of the project we are trying to estimate on some parts or the entire project that's been done before? In other words, do these parts or the whole match up? Is it the same thing? Or is just part of it the same thing?
- Is there any real performance data regarding the completed project. I mean real data such as actual financials, records of decisions and problems and obstacles, impacts, and issues.
- Is there a "lessons learned" or project review to help verify the bounds we will take from the completed project? Can we trust this information? Or was it a whitewash?
- Can other projects/undertakings be used as well?

Be wary that we must compare apples with apples here. Don't settle for "kinda" or "pretty similar." Is it the same thing or not?

Using Top Down
This technique should be called "sketching" or "bounding an estimate," but it's not. And don't confuse this with a ballpark order of magnitude. We can use this technique to produce an outline for a lower level OoM and then use the other techniques to fill in the details, apply constraints, and generally tie down the ballpark.

The general technique here is to

- Apply what's in and what's out; check what predominant pieces of work are required
- "Block things out" after identifying the predominant pieces of work that need to be done, lay them out next to each other and find the relationships between them
- Chuck some rough timelines against them; they don't have to be too accurate, but if we're using the other techniques—like expert advice—we'll be surprised at how readily rough estimates become available
- Check how confident people are with the model/outline and if they had to actually work to it.

Most of the time as PMs we should apply the other techniques at a high level or simple level of treatment to actually complete this technique—especially the two above. The application of best case/worse case polishes this technique off spectacularly.

Using Bottom Up or Detailed Estimation
This is the most onerous but most accurate form of estimation for IT projects. Sit down with each resource likely to be involved and separately map out, step by step, what they will have to do to complete the work to deliver the products in scope.

Every work day of every week should be filled, including weekends and out of hours work if appropriate. It's the only way to be sure we cover as much of the likely work as possible. But it'll map out what the work will look like at a low level, flesh out assumptions and dependencies and give us a better idea of the areas of the work that are still a bit gooey or not well known and how confident we can be with other areas.

Using Best Case/Worse Case & What If Scenarios
The best way to flesh out the bounds of reality is to apply this technique, and it's a simple one. When undertaking this technique we keep in mind that we are trying to tie down the bounds of effort and time.

While completing the above techniques we ask ourselves and the techs the following questions.

- What if that went wrong? How long would it take?
- What if that went really well? How long would it take?
- What if someone else had already done that?
- What if it couldn't be done then?
- What's the worst thing that could happen? What would it mean?

The best thing about this technique is that it will give solid boundaries for lengths of time and effort that need to be done in the best case scenario and the worse case. We can then use this information to build the appropriate OoM range of the estimate we are trying to complete.

We'll also end up with a set of scenarios, in either preparing for or completing this technique, which we can then use to set expectations for areas of likely variance—people will think we're bloody marvelous and a seer into the future—but it's just basic practice.

As an aside, that's how powerful even the adoption of the approach to using these techniques can be. They change how we think about the project and the work at hand and how we work through problems, hence they provide more rigor and better level of diligence to our project management.

Application & Assumptions

The most important note here is that we should use a mix of at least three or four if not all estimation techniques if available—or else our estimates will be off. This is because each of the approaches in the techniques above pull on the assumed reality we are trying to shape in a different way. When combined they question and challenge the other techniques and the assumptions we used with them.

We'll also end up with a list of assumptions that went into building the estimates. These are our ticket out of the gloom! Go talk to the stakeholders about them, discuss them with management, and warn of the impending doom on the dark side of the estimates as well as the benefits and good times on the brighter side of the estimates. Take them forward with us to verify and manage as risks and issues—now there's a novel idea!

Modeling a Form of Abstraction

The next thing is to understand what we are doing here. We are modeling a project management solution and building another abstraction of the project—a solution to a problem in reality (we need to get the project done). And that's what we produced a model. We call them an estimate in project management, but they are in fact a model of a way of doing things and the things to be done, to complete the scope of a project.

If we understand this, then we can apply another powerful estimating technique. Go build another model to test and prove the first one! Change the boundaries; base the next round of estimation on something different, some different set of assumptions. Don't remodel the first one with different data, but create a new model that works differently to the first one we and the techs produced.

Building Collateral

Now we've got some models, project information about other projects, and perhaps some decent lessons learnt documentation, how about bundling these things away in a safe place...wait for it...to use the next time someone asks us on Tuesday for an estimate for a complex project by the end of Friday!

Seriously, we can use this stuff over and over again, refining the material as we learn, shortening the timeframes and risk around estimation in the future.

Forecasting and Tracking

What is a forecast if not another estimate? It's simply an estimate completed while a project is running which takes into account a new variable for the estimate: what is actually happening in the project—or more precisely what has actually happened in the project in terms of its scope, time, cost, quality—amongst other things, at the point which the person making the forecast sat down to complete it.

If we want to keep track of the health of our IT projects, and I mean truly keep track of them so that reports actually mean something, then we have to maintain the same level of discipline in terms of practicing with the tools available for forecasting, that we (should have) put into the original modeling that got us to the point of starting the project in the first place.

To maintain the health of IT projects and visibility of them, we need to list a couple points here:

1. Produce accurate models of the projects in the first place (using the tools outlined in evolution of scope above) to achieve a *baseline* that is clearly visible and understood by everyone, detailing all aspects of scope delivery: effort, time, task, activities, dependencies, sequencing, and cost. This is the only way to provide a clear "starting point" we can track against.
2. Which is the next point, we have to constantly track against what we said we would do to begin with. Not change or add things arbitrarily. Yes we can update a baseline—but only formally via an approved change control system, and then we must track against the (new) baseline.
3. We have to constantly update the collateral we've built using accepted tools, to ensure that the "vision" of the project health is maintained and reflective of reality and that it is comparing apples with apples (i.e., we said we would do this and this is how we're going against what we said we would do).
4. We have to add the actuals into forecast.
5. Only when the above four points are being undertaken will (the derived) project reporting actually mean anything.

The most telling indicator of a lack of maturity in IT projects is when we only want to know, once a project is running, how much a project is going to cost and how long it will be before it's finished. What about what we are getting for the money—the scope? What are we getting? Has anything changed? Is anything occurring that is increasing or decreasing the time or cost? What did we start out to do? Are we still getting that? What's the actual value of what we are getting? Are we looking at realizing the benefits we set out to achieve? Have we realized any to date? These questions of scope delivery are just as important as those of cost and time.

Forecasting and tracking need not always be onerous, creating the minute detail we covered when forming the project. With an acceptance that project changes occur, most forecasting (if collateral is maintained, updated, and automated) can be completed extraordinarily quickly relative to the effort that went into forming the project in the first place.

Finally, if the project managers managing our IT projects are not completing the hygiene around the tools and forecasting and tracking described above, any progress reports we are reading are essentially meaningless. If basic project management practices are not occurring, like integrated forecasting, what are these reports based on? Our best guess? What we as PMs are being told to report?

Dependencies and Sequencing

When we begin to abstract the scope of a project, and document it, one of the most important aspects of this abstraction is the relationship between the parts of scope delivery we've identified. As mentioned earlier I have never seen the associated tools to identify and document these dependencies in fifteen years of IT and IT project management.

What is going on? These tools (precedence diagrams and dependency charts) coupled with the evolution of the definition of scope are prerequisites in steering a project through its course and for identifying potential problems with task sequencing, runaway timeframes, and "showstopper" events—not to mention establishing the critical path of a project.

If you work within or are affected by the sphere of IT projects or their management and you do not know what a precedence diagram or dependency chart (PM network diagram) is, how they are made, or what they are used for, stop reading this book and—if you do nothing else to improve your understanding of projects ever—research what these tools are. (Remember the dependency charts will be called network diagrams in the project management world, but they are not the network diagrams of the IT world. I can't stress this enough.)

Change is the archenemy of smooth running projects in this context, as is time. Scheduling, our most commonly (misused) and poorly constructed IT project management artifact, takes time to complete; schedules have to be updated every time something changes. Things change so rapidly that effort spent maintaining lower level schedules becomes onerous and fruitless because by the time a low level schedule has been updated—that's one where tasks have been broken down into blocks less than say five days—something else has changed and it needs to be updated again.

I frequently tell the PMs who report to me on various pieces of work not to waste time completing schedules with this lower level of task definition. Why? Because there are other tools that allow the IT PM to manage the same things as a Gantt chart does, from a different perspective, but to the same or greater effect.

For instance, creating and maintaining a low-level sequence of task milestones and their dependencies to build a dependency chart will allow greater control (rescheduling) and visibility of those tasks than a low level schedule (assuming bottom up estimates have also been completed) and will indicate where things are likely to go wrong, get delayed, or otherwise through a spanner in the works.

Coupled with a dependency driven "block" schedule—where tasks are grouped at around five days—a low-level dependency chart can manage the aspects of time with just as much minor tolerance and control as a low level schedule. Better still the dependencies are less likely to change as frequently as the timing of the tasks themselves, hence will not need to be updated as frequently, if at all.

Penultimately when heading towards production changes, because IT projects (should) have implementation plans, it's better to detail these micro-tasks at a low level in this document to manage technical and project risk than use a low level schedule. This is because it's better to see the implementation context of the risks and issues against tasks involved at this level rather than just sequencing and elapsed timeframes that will change more often than I change my underpants, which is regularly and frequently.

Finally if we as PMs need to explain, hopefully in advance, why a critical task is going to the dogs because of "other things" happening, is far easier using an A3 dependency chart than an Gantt chart with 1800 lines of tasks.

Our project managers will only know these tricks if they employ the professional tools and evolution of the definition of scope as recommended by the very project management bodies we so commonly claim to be a part of.

Cascading Terror and Abstracting the Entire Project

Generally speaking, in a project, if one aspect goes, everything goes. If scope changes so does the cost and time. If time changes so does the cost. If a quality level changes, then the time it takes to complete a review of it changes and so will the cost. If these aspects of a project are not all being managed in an integrated and accepted manner, then all hell can break loose. It only takes one uncontrolled event (by uncontrolled I mean unforeseen, unplanned for, and not handled) to push out an entire IT programme, let alone project.

If we make an addition to scope but don't account for it anywhere else, we immediately become over budget and late. If resources start doing work not "in scope," the same thing will happen. If we can't complete a task one day and the next phase of the project is dependent on it being completed—even if the task pushes out by a day—the entirety of the next phase is pushed out by at least the same amount. What if we can't complete the task for a week or a month?

Worse, if it's not immediately obvious in our 1800 line detailed schedule (Gannt chart) example from the previous section that

one minor task affects another minor task of no immediate conse-
quence, which in turn affects an important series of tasks, which
then affects something major, and so on, then VBN begins to rear its
ugly head. Even worse than worse is when our 1800 line schedule
covers only our slice of the project tasks, and (as is so commonly the
case) our delay of a week causes a vendor's schedule to go out by
two weeks, which then delays another vendor or ourselves a month
(if we include the effort to replan on the run and the subsequent
approval rounds this will trigger), and so on. Without using the commonly accepted and proven tools of managing aspects of a project's
scope delivery, we will not be able to see these cascading terrors
coming.

If we (someone) mapped the total project dependencies at the
beginning or early on in a project, then task dependencies and the
delays they can cause could be seen from that point onwards (at
the beginning of the project!). We could even build strategies and
plans for mitigating any impacts from that point onwards. No one
would yell when the wheels fall off, because the wheels would not
fall off, but they would still need oiling from time to time. Further,
without taking into account the entire landscape a project exists
within when using these tools and evolving a projects scope and
related areas, then we are equally as blind, even if we are using the
right tools.

If we don't map programme and inter-programme dependencies,
BAU and infrastructural dependencies, lead times for hardware, or
make allowances for "paint drying" time, gas depletion times, realistic document turnaround and approval times, or travel time and
other logistics, we are at the mercy of the same mechanisms that
are at play when we are not using these tools. In other words, we
end up mismanaging projects in the manner described in the project
management for IT sections above.

Acceptance Criteria: Another Abstraction of the Definition of Scope

This section has been included because the definition of acceptance criteria is another critical area where endemically poor practice seems to be occurring in IT projects.

To ease the load of our programme, delivery managers, and the poor lawyers who have to deal with the criteria we mercilessly include or accept in our IT project contracts as project managers, it needs to be stated that this next gem is *not* an acceptable acceptance criterion: signed off by the customer.

Legally as well as logically, this phrase is essentially meaningless in terms of assessing acceptance. An explanation of what acceptance criteria are and the process of acceptance, will explain why.

Acceptance criteria: a description of the bounds by which completed products/deliverables can be assessed to see whether they have been built to the agreed specification, have no faults and are fit for purpose. This includes defined parts/increments of products/deliverables, that can also be assessed for completeness.

From a project perspective, they are a description of the quality measurements to be applied and quality levels required to assess and consider a product or deliverable (successfully) complete. From a contract perspective, the acceptance process is the mechanism used to assess whether something should be paid for; this is a key concept to understand when writing up good acceptance criteria.

In this sense "signed off by the customer" is one of the last things that happens in the acceptance process, and can only happen when

- The product requirements have been clearly specified
- The criteria (the measurement methods and levels of quality) by which a product will be assessed for completeness is documented and agreed
- The person, role, or party responsible for "sign off" is documented and agreed
- The product is built
- The assessment criteria applied to the product

The last thing that usually occurs in this process is that someone pays for the work associated with building the product and in other words "signs it off."

You can see that when completing reviews and recoveries and finding acceptance criteria like "signed off by the customer" in contracts or quality related documents, we can see a raft of associated poor practices.

Each one of the steps in the wider acceptance process outlined above has its own supporting project process, each of which needs to be completed before the step can be called complete. Seeing "signed off by customer" in a document's acceptance criteria immediately tells reviewers that at the very least, the second and third steps above have not been understood or completed. At worst it tells us that

- The parties involved are not applying good project management.
    - o As well defined acceptance criteria are one of the outputs of the evolution of the definition of scope
    - o All the parties involved accepted the poor acceptance criteria

- Not only is the contract at risk, but all parties involved are as well.
- Project delivery and success criteria will be vague, will not lend themselves to critical legal assessment, and will not quickly resolve contract conflicts.

This is a pretty poor state for a project to be in, whether it's a fifty thousand or five million dollar project.

When project reviewers find "signed off by customer" defined as acceptance criteria in project documentation, it indicates to us that the quality of project management practice we will expect to find elsewhere during the project review will be as equally bad. In these situations we typically find that

- Requirements have not been specified or will be vague and not "signed off" or agreed upon.
- Scope will not be defined to a level where we can use it to produce a project's products.
- Evidence of bad project habits such as scope creep, gold plating, and missing deliverables will be found.
- There will be a basic disagreement between parties about what was to be done.
- Supporting PMOs will not be mature or processes will have been interfered with (as they let these "acceptance criteria" through contract review, if they reviewed them at all), so project reporting will not be accurate or based on "reality."
- Supporting SDLCs and IT practices will not be mature or will have also been interfered with because requirements and quality definitions (including acceptance criteria) are artifacts of good IT practice.
- Unless absolutely no one knows what's going on, which is unlikely, and if those responsible for getting a project to this

stage are still around, there will still be "vagaries" appearing in all sorts of project documents and emails[8]

In this sense, a contract, even if it's between two parties of the same organisation in the form of a project charter or brief, is often a far better indicator of a project's health than the latest status report.

Defining Acceptance Criteria
Defining acceptance criteria is actually hard to do.

It's literally a process of describing something that doesn't exist yet, without using terms which describe what the thing that doesn't exist actually is, and only using only terms that describe when we will know that we are "happy" with the thing that will exist, once it is built or delivered.

So as a generic introduction to real acceptance criteria here are some examples.

---

8 Now some of you may be thinking that when we find the individuals responsible, they get taken out back and shot. If only it was that easy—well you know what I mean. Many times the people hiding their mistakes are just outright scared and have got themselves into more than a bit of a pickle and a tangle.

Commonly they may be hiding things out of loyalty to peers and managers. They won't be "criminals" or intentional saboteurs. Their own PMOs or managers are likely to have let them down by creating a situation, due to poor process or lack of backing, whereby something as critical as acceptance criteria have not a snowball's chance in hell of ever being defined accurately. These people are normally carrying huge stress loads related to their work and the mess that it's in.

The relief is clearly evident when these situations are resolved, and there is a great sense of fulfillment in terms of completing a review/recovery when maturity is shown in resolving the situation; which benefits the poor sods trying to cope with the mess.

We don't often find the stereotypical "idiot" or "muppet" that shouldn't be allowed to do their jobs. Project management is more complicated than this; rarely in my experience (thankfully) have the culprits responsible been negligent, actively working against the organisation or undertaking intentional criminal activity.

Product/ Deliverable	Acceptance Criteria	Notes
Design Documentation	Will be deemed complete when: • It is documented to the extent whereby it could be reasonably implemented within *relevant environment*; and • As such it has been approved by *ABC Tech People*	The design has to be approved by the technical body requiring it, before it is accepted ('approved') at a project level.
Bill of Materials	Will be deemed complete once it has been enumerated to the extent that it materially reflects the necessary requirements for *a proposed environment*, (*and should be*) based on approved design documentation.	This is good because it will hold the people responsible to produce a more accurate BoM, which reflects the work that has been asked for. If an accurate BoM can't be produced, this is a good thing, as the design obviously isn't express enough— so we shouldn't be building stuff yet, or approving associated products/deliverables

Product/ Deliverable	Acceptance Criteria	Notes
XYZ Presentation	Will be deemed complete when the presentation material has been produced and the presentation event has taken place; and when the material and event produces *outcome 123*.	Pedantic maybe, it's just a presentation after all, but accurate and concise, and needed—as we will have to pay for the effort that goes into the presentation. The purpose of the presentation material and the event itself is to achieve some desired outcome—while outcomes may be somewhat subjective (engagement, buy in), regardless they need to be defined and agreed.
Implementation Plan	Will be deemed complete when: • It is documented to the extent whereby it can reasonably demonstrate rigor around the implementation of the design in the *relevant environments*; and • As such it has been approved by *ABC Tech People*	The term "rigor" in context of the implementation plan would have to be defined somewhere, in an associated contract or quality plan, or as reference to standards the change body associated with delivery has produced. And it's the same as the design documentation above; the implementation plan needs to be approved by the technical body receiving it into change management, before it is accepted at a project or contract level.

Product/ Deliverable	Acceptance Criteria	Notes
An Implementation	Will be deemed complete when: • It is demonstrable that the implementation materially reflects the approved design; and • is functionally fit for purpose	An implementation of anything has to be tied to the design supporting the work and products—else we shouldn't be doing it. Also the assessment of fit for purpose is a statement which means that the intention of an associated contract, and any scope definition—including requirements—will hold anyone building things for us, to build things: • that actually work as desired • that were actually asked for
"As-Built" Documentation	Will be deemed complete when it is enumerated to the extent that it demonstrably reflects the accepted implementation and to *specified management practices*.	A note here that it will be project technical staff that know whether the "as built" reflects what has been built. So this should be accepted by the project for approval—as in theory nothing should be handed over to BAU at the point in time when we are assessing as built documentation for completeness. The specified management practices will need to be specified somewhere in the same document as the acceptance criteria, or in a reference to another document or standard. The definition of acceptable will also be dependent on the final purpose of the documentation, and whether or not BAU require procedural material included in their "as built" documentation.

These generic acceptance criteria need to be taken with a pinch of salt. In other words don't just blindly copy them into your project documents. I've provided them as a general introductory and inverse example to the "signed off by customer" level of acceptance criteria.

The trick is to know what it is that we are delivering first, what it will look like when it's finished, and have this defined well. Then building acceptance criteria is just a matter of deciding what standards and kind of standards and methods will or can be used to measure (see) if something has been delivered (built) successfully.

Yet again the thorough and complete definition of requirements is a key factor to project success and a prerequisite to building sound acceptance criteria. If you're using SCRUM or PRINCE2, the contractual acceptance criteria may need to be tied and aggregated to the detailed product descriptions or user stories, so may not look exactly like the above. However, all acceptance criteria should describe the measure of acceptance and the process of applying that measure.

How Do we Know We're Done?

When all the scope has been delivered to the agreed quality and acceptance criteria, a project is finished.

If we aren't tracking, monitoring, and assessing how the delivery of accepted and approved scope is going, we can never tell if we have finished or whether we missed something. If we keep adding more things to do in an uncontrolled manner—a manner that doesn't involve the assessment and agreement of those additions, and a probable subsequent change to the business case—then we have an unending project that we cannot assess for success.

How Do We Know We're Successful?

When all the scope has been delivered to agreed quality and acceptance criteria and to the agreed budget in the agreed timeframes within accepted tolerances, we have delivered a successful project.

Only when all the benefits as stated in the business case have been realized is the initiative (and hence the project which supported it) considered successful. As the majority of IT projects and their associated business cases never actually get reviewed against the benefits realization and relationship to the objectives those benefits were meant to achieve; they are never truly successful. This is the real circle of IT project life and this is not flippancy or "being clever" in terms of assessing a project for success.

The failure of IT projects is an all encompassing nightmare for businesses and organisations that never truly get to achieve the benefits these IT systems were meant to bring them. There are so many areas related to IT project management lacking good practice, against all levels of an organization, that (as I've said before) I'm astounded there aren't more tragic IT project failures that can't be covered up.

This is another key point to consider.

Although we hear about the super-failures in the media, the project "near misses" are more common than the super-failures and are so common that a consultant told me that their practice even had their own (internal) pet name for them: super-hyper-mega-misses. These were so common that part of their practice now included reviews focusing solely on identifying the system-configurations left by or intended for implementation by projects, and associated poor processes and practices that caused them.

Remember what we are seeing in the media is only the tip of the iceberg, the project failures that leak out and make the news. The tangled mess of "administration" and poor practice does not commonly make news headlines. Projects managed in this way—combined—cost organisations more than all the super-failures put together. How many $30k projects can we really afford to come in at $75k or $100k? How many projects can we really afford to have delivered only 50 percent of the functionality that was stated originally?

Project management, especially in IT, needs to be considered a profession or career, not a job; we can't continue to just show up and complete "office administration" and expect these behemoths to be successful.

IT Parallels in Abstraction

I mentioned previously that I've found I apply many of the tools and approaches I was taught in computer science and information systems theory to the projects that I undertake. This is because there are some tight parallels between the analytical aspects of the two disciplines and I think they are useful to all IT PMs without a background in formal IT. Also, there are some direct parallels between the life cycles of the two disciplines I want to outline here, mainly because it's foundation or prerequisite knowledge for everyone involved or affected by IT projects.

I'm providing this section as a reminder or introductory pointer to other resources.

Methods of Abstraction

Defining Problem Spaces and Solutions

The following were the first "lessons" in information systems and computer science.

- Problems and in IT are, more often than not, complex.
- Complex problems cannot be managed without using specialized approaches and processes.
- While many of these approaches and processes may be intuitive they still have to be taught, learnt and applied appropriately.
- There are better ways to manage certain complex things that have been successful in the past. These ways or methods are called algorithms.

These are the "facts of life" for IT; it is complex and its projects can be even more so. The quicker everyone at all organizational levels accepts this, the easier IT project management will become.

We have to take our ego out of the mix to be successful in IT. We need to accept that there are people out there with far greater brains than ours who have already come up with the ways of doing things that are far more efficient and prone to success than we can possibly come up with by ourselves—like problem and solution definition.

The most basic and successful method for resolving a complex problem is as follows:

1. Problem Definition: Fully define the problem (thing) that is at hand. Make sure you know what it is you are dealing with first!
2. Solution Definition:
   a. Develop a solution to meet the defined problem. Make sure you are coming up with something to fix the problem, the whole problem, and nothing but the problem!
   b. Decide whether it's worth doing something.
   c. Prescribe an approach to implementation of the solution which will resolve the problem—defining a solution doesn't implement it or always provide an approach to implement it.
   d. Decide whether it's still worth doing something.
3. Implement a solution. In this context, a project is the implementation of a defined solution to resolve an individual or organization's defined problem. Yet again, it's (literally) one of the last things we should be doing...first!
4. Check that the implemented solution resolved the problem. If not, return to step one and try to improve the previous steps.

In the broadest sense, the entire system development lifecycle (SDLC—see below) is built on the premise of problem/solution definition above. The general flow of a project in every formal project management lifecycle follows or is parallel to this successful approach to complex problem management. (See SDLC and Project Lifecycles below.) This is no accident; is this method not another instance of the PDCA cycles already discussed previously? Is this not another parallel to describing the evolution of an IT project's scope? And do the steps above not read like a reworded and paralleled version of PRINCE2's business case theme?

This is often the most frustrating thing for me I face in IT project management. So many good people have come up with so many proven ways and successful ways of doing IT project management. Yet it seems the majority of us either aren't aware of them or don't use the things we've learnt and have qualifications in. This is why a few years back, a "strategic program manager" could say to me that they didn't see the need to produce an integrated "programme plan" (consolidated schedule of projects) to establish a "pipeline view" (a view of all work and the relationships between them in the programme) because four out of fifty projects were yet to be defined; so there was no point building a programme schedule for the other forty-six! What fresh hell is this? The combined "active" portion of the programme was worth around $10M. I even offered to create the programme schedule for free because I knew establishing this kind of view would instantly provide a view of the programme's risk in terms of dependencies between projects, overlaping work, showstopping events, bottlenecks, and the general size of the programme itself. They declined.[9]

We are lucky that the successful methods of defining complex problems and their solutions have already been, themselves, defined, and

9   The reason for this seemingly idiocy became apparent as this particular contract progressed. It seems the PgM had been used to running things their way for years until an incoming PMO manager called a restructure and hauled the PgM and their unit into line, and close to the activities of the PMO. Establishing a programme view would have been yet another removal of control and power from the PgM, by making this view available to all who needed it. The motivations of people in IT project management are wide, varied and destructive—always check them out.

proven. We need to accept that the successful path of success has been blazed before we got here. The real trick is in applying these algorithms in any given instance of reality. In other words, use them in our working lives as IT project managers.

Project Moral: things in IT can be very complex (read expensive). Get over it and, IT PMs, get ready to communicate this in detail.

Project Moral: don't reinvent the wheel. If you are making something up as you go along (not using or adapting defined and accepted IT and project processes, approaches, methods), you're doing it wrong. End of story.

Un-solvability and Intractability

Are you prepared for the bad news? Are you sitting down? Because successful project management does involve delivering bad news to people, even on the best-run projects, so here it goes. Some problems cannot be solved. This is a special note to CIOs, business managers, and IT operations managers. This includes business problems (of which IT provides many automated solutions). More commonly, some IT solutions to business problems are just too complex to be practical or too expensive to implement. There's actually a term for this: intractable.

When a problem is intractable it generally doesn't have a realistic or practical solution that can be implemented in real life. This is a handy concept to know about when we are asked for a magic fix that will, with a single-logon, make an exec's iPad talk to every service in the business, from home, without compromising security, while at the same time allowing their teenage son or daughter to use social networking, without having to log out.

Intractability is also something to be mindful of as we are developing estimates for a project. A solution may have been outlined already, but the constituent parts that cost money to implement and the relationship between those parts will not have been discovered, let alone detailed. Any number of external environmental factors may also nullify the embryonic solution (i.e., network connectivity limitations or lack of documentation), while it is being detailed via the project establishment and its estimation techniques. Better practice would be to thoroughly define the problem and potential solutions before getting too far down the track, and definitely before the expectation that a solution can be implemented (and an associated project established or even begun) has been lodged in customer's/ management's minds.

Project Moral: sometimes the best thing you can do for your customer or client is to nicely decline a request—also known as "saying no" —providing full knowledge of the reasons why something is intractable and why you are declining.

Managing Complexity

How do we start to define the seemingly indefinable monster called a problem, let alone a solution to it?

Along with general analysis skills like interviewing and abstraction to produce diagrams, the best way of dealing with defining something complex is to take the "thing" to be defined—in this instance an IT problem, solution, or project—and break it down into its component parts, noting the relationship between those parts as we go even if we have to define those component parts ourselves. There are several techniques for doing this, but the prime two are top down analysis and bottom up analysis, commonly grouped under a method called decomposition.

Decomposition

Decomposition is not what happens to a project when it dies. Briefly, decomposition runs like this.

1. Sketch out at a high level the very boundaries of the problem.
    a. Have a good think about what is part of the problem, what looks like it's part of the problem but isn't, and what is just hanging around the boundaries but not remotely related to it.
    b. Find the questions that are being asked around the problem. Why can't I do this? Why isn't this working? Inherent within the answers will be the goals or objectives that someone is trying to achieve in trying to find a solution to their problem, and hence, a better definition of the problem itself.
2. Now within this problem, see if the whole can be broken down into logical parts, noting both the relationship to the whole a part has and the relationship between the parts at this level.
3. Take one of the parts and complete step two again, breaking the part down into further parts noting the relationships of the decomposed parts to its parent part, the whole, and all other parts at all levels.
4. Keep decomposing or breaking down the parts until they seem logically manageable and easily understandable. Logical in this sense is related to the goals and objectives that have been identified in step one. In other words, until the parts have been defined in the context of problem itself.

Then

5. To add rigor to the process, take the parts on the lowest level and detail them to the nth degree. Rebuilding any high level relationships and parts as the detailing of the lower level parts are completed.
6. Do step five, altering high levels as you go until you have covered all parts within the problem including the whole.

What you will have done on completion is modeled the problem space, the space in which all relevant things to the problem have been identified.

Steps one to four are the "top down" method of analysis because we started at the top and worked our way down. Steps five and six are the "bottom up" method of analysis because we started at the bottom, detailing everything we could, and worked our way upwards to the highest level. This challenges the hidden vagaries that come with our top down analysis. It is important to note that we must be mindful not to model the solution before trying to define the problem. Until we know what the problem is, we can't create a solution that will meet the problem.

This may seem irrelevant to project management, but it's not. Firstly, there are direct parallels to the accepted project management techniques including estimating, creating schedules, iteration through the definition of scope and related project management tools (such as requirements, dependency charts (network diagrams), and WBS/PBS structures), therefore this type of analysis is in fact predominantly used throughout most of the project management techniques and tools—and should be—when employing them.

As such, IT project managers should have a thorough, if not formal, grounding in decomposition or top down and bottom up analysis.

Secondly, because this method is a "generic" algorithm for successful definition of problems, it's not limited to IT or the project management tools that use the method as mentioned above. It can be applied to any project problem. What is a problem if not another name for issue? What if there are highly complex risks in a project? Wouldn't adopting a proven method (outside of quantification and in support of qualification)[10] instead of using the best guess

---

10 If you don't know what the qualification and quantification of risks are, or the difference between them, go look it up on the Internet, as they are another basic project management tool for managing risks in a project.

approaches make a project manager and the project they manage more successful?

Finally, I bet most of you have actually used this method already, without knowing it. If you have produced a mind map or been part of a group producing one, then you have already employed the method of decomposition. A mind map is one type of diagram that we use to document the abstraction that the decomposition method produces.

Project Moral: when faced with something complex or tough during a project, PMs should always break it down in a structured way to get a better understanding of it and hence better control over it.

Grouping, Hierarchies, and Venn Diagrams
Just when you thought you'd never use them outside of school, a section including Venn diagrams!

Seriously though, at the beginning of this section I made a statement regarding the absolute necessity for project managers to be able to manage multidimensional abstractions. It s part of the territory of the project manager and in this section I cover some of the most basic methods of defining abstractions that are included in project management, all of which are covered in information systems or computer science theory, and some of which are taught at school and all of which revolve around grouping things together.

Identifying like things and separating out things that are not alike, applying structure to these things to create hierarchies, and not-ing any overlaps between the groupings are basic skills required of project managers.

The project management technique of activity and task identifica-tion is a basic tool that uses these methods. The resulting work breakdown structures are a hierarchical view of these tasks and activities, in other words, groupings. As is risk identification and management, identifying and applying appropriate treatments to stakeholder groups, and periodic reporting—covering project things grouped by time periods. The identification and management of schedule overlaps between two or more tasks/task groups, and the resulting resource coordination that goes with it, is a critical skill that has parallels, if not roots, in the Venn theory of relationship identification, and even more abstractly for projects, is then applied across time.

The point here is to draw attention to the fact that none of the things mentioned above appear in that list of administration tasks I included in the "process is as process does or not" section. All of these skills or methods are all taught either at school or at university, and used daily in professional project management.

Project Moral: project management should be treated as a profession or a career with its accepted practices and techniques widely known and used.

The Pointer Sisters—My Favorite Parallel Algorhythm

For some strange and twisted reason, one of the things I enjoyed most during my years of computer science was the creation and manipulation of low-level data structures. Takes all sorts I guess. Believe it or not, one of these data structures taught me an invaluable lesson about project management.

Everyone knows that computers run via their computer programmes and that programmes are logical sets of instructions that do things to make a computer and its applications like Microsoft Word work. A pointer is a basic type of data used in programming, the sole purpose of which is to point to something else, normally another piece or set of data. That's its job. It doesn't hold any data and isn't used for anything else but to point to something else within the computer programme. On its own it is a useless thing, which ironically can be said about any other type of grouped data—whether it's text, numeric, or other type of data—without the inclusion of pointers.

You see, the thing is the programmes that run on our computers are made up of families of different types of data that are related, like for instance an employee record. This would have text data for the name and role of an employee, and numeric data to hold the employee's ID number and salary, and maybe even a BLOB (binary large object) like a photo of the employee (a large object in computer terms), held in the computer's memory as millions and millions of zeros and ones (or as binary, hence the term BLOB).

All these families are housed in the computer's memory when the computer is running, and the memory is made up of lots of addresses, just like street addresses in a city. Each "family" of data (in our example, an employee record) has its own address just like house addresses we use for our homes.

In real life, until someone gave you an address of someone or a shop for instance, you could not travel there. It's the same for computer programmes. Without something pointing out where these employee records are, we cannot find them.

Enter the pointer. The only thing a pointer stores is the address of something else, which can be the start of a list and the end of a list if need be. If I include a pointer or two in an employee record I can immediately find an employee record and sort the employee records. In fact, I can find and retrieve any data about an individual employee or a group of employees and build a list of employees by moving from one employee to the next just by using or following the addresses the pointers each employee record holds. So with this relational type of data suddenly the employees' records are retrievable and in context, and so are useable or valuable.

This may be a long-winded way to the lesson I learned, but it's worth it. Like an employee record in the example above, in project management, unless we are holding the information about how something relates to everything else in a project, that something, whether it is an issue, a task, a contract, a scope definition, or anything in project management is useless to us *unless its project context is also known*.

Also, if we aren't holding the item's complete relational information (how everything in the project relates to it), then it's worse than useless; it's misleading or outright dangerous. This is because we cannot make meaningful and sound decisions about projects based on incomplete information or information that does not take everything about the project into account. Projects are not linear; they don't follow a straightforward path. They are multidimensional beasts with every project aspect relating to every other project aspect. This is another facet of the "cascading terror" section discussed above.

It is common for project managers to make decisions based on partial information, having not "taken everything into account," and then spend a great deal of energy and effort trying to fix the issues and problems the decision has caused, as impacts that weren't seen at the time of making the decision begin to occur.

This concept is most evident in precedence mapping where the dependencies of phases, stages, tasks, and activities are identified and documented, but this type of relational analysis can and should be applied across all aspects of a project.

Have you ever been in a meeting where the person ultimately responsible for a project delivery is asking basic progress assessment questions and expecting concise answers in return? But the project manager in question can't explain concisely where they are in a project without going into some great detail about how they are dealing with an issue. With every long-winded explanation, the delivery manager becomes more and more frustrated as the project manager fails to answer the delivery manager's simple and fairly standard questions. This happens because the project manager has lost the "holistic" relational overview of their project. This type of relational view of a project can only be established and maintained by using the techniques outlined in the evolution of scope section above—not by completing administration tasks.

Project Moral: it's just as important in project management to identify and manage the relationships between the logical groupings of project things, as it is the things within those groupings.

Project Moral: always verify information first, its source, its accuracy, and how it relates to the project in total before acting upon it.

The Automation Boundary and Reason for IT

There is a fundamental parallel to the automation boundary decision in IT and the reasoning for doing IT projects in the first place.

The automation boundary, while sounding like something out of a robot science fiction movie, is in fact much more mundane. It's the boundary at which a decision regarding a problem in the real world is better off solved using real human beings, rather than automating a solution via a computer system or systems.

If something can be done cheaper and more efficiently by a human being, or if it is too abstract a task or process for a computer to undertake, then the rule of thumb is—don't automate it.

This automation boundary check-point is fundamental to forming business cases for IT systems that have a chance of success. It's a fundamental question that should be applied for every proposed solution to a real world problem. An example may help here.

A few years ago, I was doing some consultancy for a small business that had come up with a template solution to a problem in their specific industry. What they had asked for was a computer system (automated way in which) to produce these templates for their various clients. As we modeled their associated business plan it became evident that the level of investment required up front was significantly more than the number clients buying the product would return in the first few years of the product's life. So I produced a model whereby a full-time employee could complete the production and meet the demand over the first few years, as the system was built incrementally. In other words it was cheaper to hire a capable bloke or lass to make the template solutions in the first two years, than it was to build an entire computer system to do it.

In terms of the automation boundary this solution started out with humans doing the tasks, and gradually increased the automation—or involvement of a computer based solution, and did not cross the boundary entirely until a few years down the track.

The parallel to projects here is that fundamental questioning of what we are doing and why we are doing it, and even "are we doing the right thing?" It's a principal practice supported by all the project management bodies.

Before hurtling down the track, hell for leather, we always need to ask what is we are doing, why we are doing it, and if there are any better ways of do it than what is currently under consideration.

Project Moral: Always ask why are we doing this, is it the right thing to do, and is there a better way of doing it?

Direct Parallels: The Project Life Cycle and its Relationship to the Systems Development Life Cycle

The main point to start with here is that there is a direct parallel with the lifecycle of a system and its development, and the project lifecycle, and project managers and architects especially need to be aware of it. If architects want their conceptual plans to become reality, then they will need a project to do it. If project managers want projects to run then they'll need architects to form the technical bounds for the subsequent development. On the technical side a business will need both these roles to work together early on to successfully get something of the ground in the first place—else the initiative will forever be a wounded albatross. Unfortunately, the duality of responsibility mainly is worn by the project manager.

If it was an ideal world, filled with fluffy bunnies and butterflies, and chocolate, and gnomes, and pixies, and chocolate gnomes, and flying chewing gum cars, and just

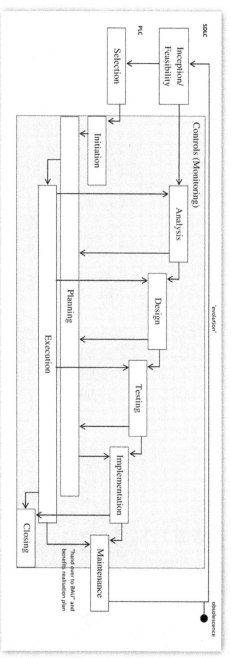

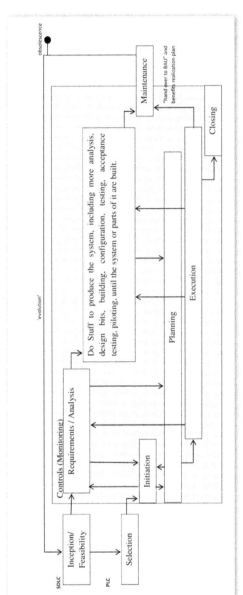

everything, the diagram on page 167 would be what the relationship between the system development lifecycle and project lifecycle would look like. This is would be what the traditional "waterfall" approach would be like and how projects supported it. But it's not an ideal world...

For a start there is no singularly accepted lifecycle for all systems, there are hundreds of variations, for hundreds of various (good) reasons. A more commonly used and generalized SDLC and "blue skies" relationship to the PLC would be as per the diagram on page 168.

But even this is too good to be true and commonly looks like the diagram on page 169.

This is more commonly accurate, start from an embryonic idea, jump straight into a statement of work or delivery contract, remember that it should be run as a project and retrospectively apply the "administration" form of project management, half way through completing it replace the PM and some key technical staff, don't ever close (stop) the project; just take unending scope modifications because "it's not working in BAU," and never really hand all of its products over for maintenance—at least until it's too late for BAU folk to object. And conceptually it gets worse (or better depending on whether you are a glass half full or a glass half empty person).

The relationships between the PLC—and appropriate application of project management practices—and different versions of a SDLC vary as well, depending on the initiative the project will support and the type of SDLC at hand; for instance a really complex initiative with much uncertainty and great risk, could have several projects which will manage that uncertainty by taking a single SDLC phase and break down implementation into smaller chunks, in theory like the diagram on 170.

Or...if you were developing a complex product using "SCRUM-like" or tightly iterative development processes, the SDLC and PLC relationship in theory could look something like the diagram on 171.

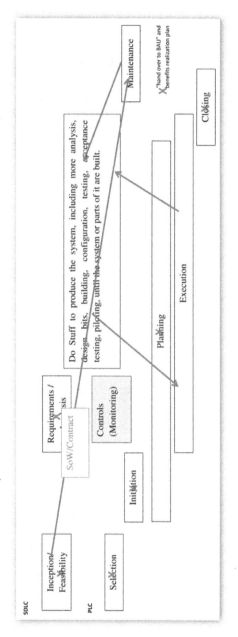

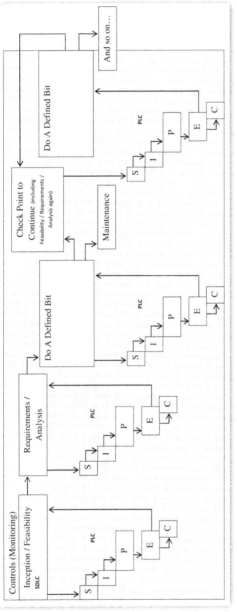

And it goes on, with almost endless combinations depending on the type of system at hand, uncertainty and risk, the business appetite for either of them, and the maturity of the ICT group supporting the initiative; and the maturity of the PMO group and project manager(s) supporting the initiative's project(s).

The point here is that someone—project managers (especially senior project managers)—must be able to, not only adapt their project management practice appropriately to the situation, but also be able to tell a) What SDLC, if any, they are dealing with or is appropriate for the initiative and its upcoming project, b) where the whole process is in terms of the SDLC and PLC, c) whether or not crucial bits of collateral or steps from either camp have or will be missed, and d) what to do about problems.

The reason for this is that in practice, it is highly unlikely that any other resource type in ICT will understand in detail the SDLC and PLC and the relationship between the two. I hear cries that, "in theory," our consultants, architects, CIOs, line managers, or programme managers will understand—just chill out, Dave." In reality, I say architects rarely if ever have project management skills; consultants are actually technical engineers and consultants in name only (see architect comment previously). CIOs are too busy, line managers are too busy or not interested, and commonly ICT programme managers don't have technical knowledge or, more importantly, won't even have actual project management skills that the IT industry expects them to have.

So I ask, "Who in our projects is actually managing this integration area?" Not "In theory, who in our projects is actually managing this integration area?" That is a completely different question.

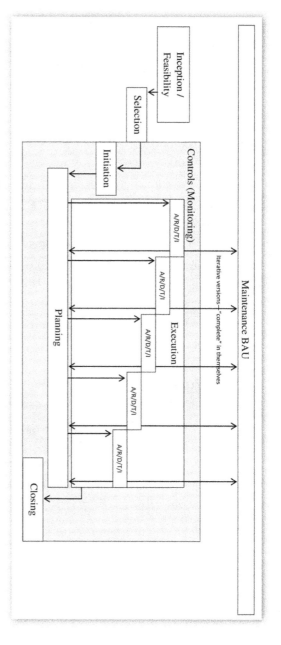

Then I hear from my project manager peers that my "technical lead" will take care of this for me and that I need not have any experience in the industry specific area I manage projects in. "It would be beneficial, but not necessary." Pah and bah humbug! Most IT projects don't have a single technical lead. People are busy and resource is expensive. If we have a "technical lead" on our projects, they are also undertaking technical work and too focused to maintin a holistic technical view for their PM. More importantly, technical leads are made up from the grouping of roles listed above and will suffer from the limitations noted.

No matter how many times we read in a lessons learned documentation that a technical lead from start-to-finish would have been a good idea. Well duh! We are still not getting or retaining them. I say this to my particularly "bright eyed and busy tailed" project management peers who have a textbook answer for everything. Damn your eyes and stop making naive statements. At present, in IT project management, it not only helps if you have a technical background as a project manager, it's a prerequisite for delivering successful IT projects.

Change Again

Let's map these lifecycles into the context of the outside world (the business) the information technology groups we employ to enable the technology and change over time (as per the diagram on page 173). We'll get a picture of those levels of change that can affect an IT initiative and its associated projects mentioned in earlier sections, and hence that must be managed to ensure successful projects.

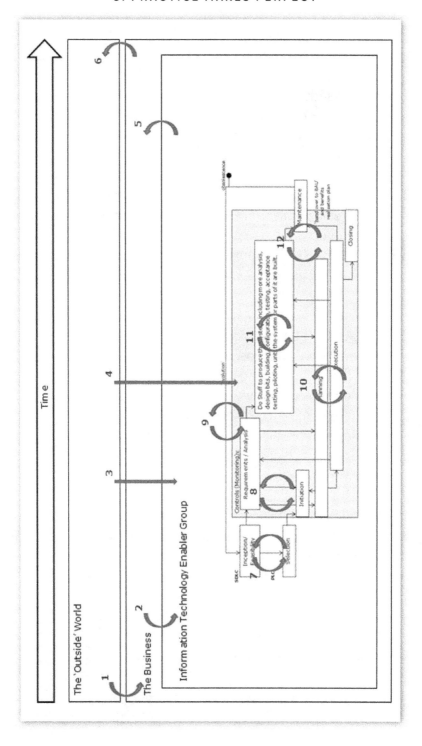

1) The world and the business change point: We need to remember that the outside world is what our organisations interact with. As such, changes in market dynamics, customer needs, laws, government, and government policies, as well as the industries whose products and services our organisations provide, are significant drivers for change in our business.

These "external drivers" give rise to changes required in how the business operates and what it needs to deliver to stay competitive or serve its citizens; hence, there will be flow on affects for our IT initiatives and their projects as the business adapts to these drivers—sometimes that's midway through a project!

2) The business and IT change point: This describes pressures, organisational changes, needs, wants, objectives, money, timeframes, and expectations of our organisation itself, and its interaction with the IT body or groups that support it. It's key to remember the critical relationship between IT and the business. The business asks IT to automate its business processes so that it can remain flexible, competitive, or efficient in delivering its services and products.

Hence, this is a significant formal channel for change in IT projects as the business "asks" for new initiatives, but also a just as significant channel for change as the business changes its mind such as through restructures and new management.

These first two change points can be so significant in their impacts that they can completely erase the raison d'etre for an IT project in a matter of months or even weeks.

3) IT industry change point for IT enablers: This is the driver from the external IT industry and its changes in technologies

and practices that directly influence and change the internal architectures and technologies used to support business automation, supported on behalf of the business by the internal IT enablers.

This creeping change often presents itself as solution, programme, and even environmental obsolescence; the length of time it takes to complete technology projects, in terms of infrastructure programmes and their objectives and the (aging) solutions that are being implemented by IT projects, is a critical delivery factor.

It is crucial to be mindful of, track, and manage the change impacts of time in this sense for every IT project.

4) IT industry change point for IT projects: Almost the inverse of the above change point is where a new technology has to be introduced as part of or all of the solution an IT project is implementing. The project becomes the overt change agent for this new technology. For some reason this change agent is often a nasty surprise to architects within the IT enabler group, both in terms of the mandate the project has to implement the technology, and often the introduction of the technology itself, which has flow on effects within the environment where the solution is being implemented.

The impacts of these effects are coupled with change point nine—project interaction with the IT group; it is a technology change that must be managed by the project the moment the technology is confirmed. Questions should be asked such as; does it fit with the rest of the architecture? Are there IT staff to manage it in terms of skills and staff numbers? What other systems, architecture, and architectural direction will it impact? A project implementing a new technology should ensure the mapping and communication of the associated technical change footprint has been covered.

The project may also be made responsible for the implementations related to the technical change footprint; but, decisions regarding whether this would be a valid increase can only be made if the associated programme(s) and enterprise architecture representatives are aware of the following: when the new technology is coming in, what it is, and what it means for the present architecture.

5) IT and the business change point: It seems obvious that this point where change occurs (in the form of new or updated systems for the business to consume) needs special management, but it's often overlooked. This is where our project efforts actually affect a real human being in the business (as opposed to us IT people who apparently aren't real human beings in this model).

Communications and positioning them to come from the right business area is a key success factor when delivering systems to the business. In effect, we are going to "move someone's cheese" when we implement a new system. As such, it is imperative that the messaging regarding the associated "business change" is appropriate and comes from the right place.

IT rarely, if ever, owns the initiative making intentional business change via its projects and the systems they implement or modify. IT is always acting on behalf of some business group and its initiative even if the actual change is a technical change such as a maintenance patch, upgrade, or security modification to remove a vulnerability. Most importantly, a technical change *always* has an associated business change footprint, no matter how small.

It is the project's responsibility (and therefore sponsorship or executive management's responsibility) to ensure that the business change associated with the technical delivery is as well defined as the technical change. The project should also ensure that communication material and plans associated with the initiative and its business change have been produced, and that they align to the technical communications plan, and be owned by the business that is making the business change associated with the incoming technical change (system or modification).

Failure to manage this change point gets IT in hot water makes for grumpy business staff and management and further erodes what trust IT and project management has built within the business.

6) IT and the outside world change point: Sometimes we run a project that implements an external interface—something customers or citizens can interact with directly—on behalf of the business. Uh oh! We better get this right! What was said for the above change point can be said here too with two important notes.

The business change that requires management is a change for customers or citizens who do not care about our IT or project woes at all. They are expecting only the maintenance or improvement of the existing service from the body providing the interface into its systems. As such, if this change point is not managed then any adverse effects are public and will likely damage the reputation of the organisation concerned, or directly lose them custom.

Project Change Points 7, 8, 10, 11, and 12) These change points have been discussed in this book whether it's the issues around getting the project off the ground in the first place (7), the iterations and changes of requirements for a project, its scope definition, and subsequent initiation (8), the changes and impacts that occur when planning and managing the execution or delivery of a project's scope (10), the things that go wrong and changes that occur when we actually try to do things (11), and the change that occurs near or at the end of the project when the products its delivered are handed into BAU, the contracts used to deliver it are closed down, any project reviews undertaken, and the structures which formed the "project" are dismantled (12).

9) IT Enabler Group and the Project: I separated this one because we need to be mindful that this "change point" masks a raft of actual change points. This includes what we commonly refer to as "change Management" in our IT projects, and pretty much the only change area we seem to focus on and spend inordinate amounts of time in as IT project managers. Hopefully this section and its diagram can once and for all put IT projects in the context of the enormous breadth and depth of change in which they actually have to be managed.

This change management area also includes interactions with any IT subgroup that can be or is effected by, or which can or will affect an IT project. Including

- BAU staff and vendors and the way they openly and clearly communicate all their patching frequencies, backup regimes, and other impacts to change windows.
- Architects and the open and transparent way they indicate the latest update to associated enterprise environmental plan and initiatives, and their impacts.
- Other programmes, projects, and vendors—including working on the same projects—and the seamless way we all interact and communicate our schedules, impacts, and other "gotchas"

Just for clarification, I am being sarcastic in this list and the things I have said occur in a positive way—don't.

As you would expect keeping across this maelstrom of "change" is a key aspect of delivering successful IT projects.

13) IT and the business change point: This is something we need to be especially mindful of. It's not just our IT projects that impact the business, but other aspects of IT, including IT related processes, the service desk, and its direct daily interaction with the business, maintenance impacts, and outages.

These items all have an effect on the IT project we run. Whether it's in a good way resulting from good service, or in a bad way because the changes we want to make are riding on the back of a week of major outages and adverse impacts on the business; the IT projects we run are first and foremost seen as IT.

Also taken in conjunction with change point two, this is where the rubber meets the road in terms of the assessment and realization of benefits the business was expecting, when it started the initiative which formed and approved an IT project in the first place. Whether IT got it right in the end is directly related to what it was asked to do in the first place, and how well the IT project continually translated that request, via the evolution of the definition of scope, and the implementation of both the project lifecycle and adherence to an appropriate system development lifecycle.

14) The business and the outside world change point: This change point is really about the strategies, programmes, and initiatives the business put in place to interact with its customer or citizens. Coupled with the first change point where the business reacts to incoming drivers for change, there will be many outward flowing programmes or initiatives to

try and preemptively influence or keep pace alongside the incoming influences and constraints the business needs to field.

Similar to the first change point, there will be flow on affects for our IT initiatives and their projects should the business decide to or need to change its outgoing strategies for interaction, and the programmes and initiatives it has put in place to shape that inter- action—again sometimes that will be midway through a project!.

Like the change point above, this is also a benefits assessment area where initiatives—and the projects that delivered products to achieve the objectives set within those initiatives—will be assessed to see if they were actually successful.

I can hear cries that its architects, CIOs, programme, and business managers that take care of these things as well as the project man- ager within the sphere of the project. Again I point out that the majority of our IT projects are failing and it's largely because these change points aren't being managed, that people do not have the awareness to manage them in the context of projects and their own roles, and it is the project managers that end up dealing with these levels of change. We need PMs to be aware of all levels of change and armed with skills to counter it.

Because our IT groups and PMO structures don't spend time integrating theses lifecycles (and hence have lifecycles that don't relate properly or at all), the associated start-up and initiating pro- cesses are often messy, confusing, and lend themselves to delays as different roles insist on different checkpoints before continuing. Including

- The CIO or Ops manager who wants to shape budget from another area, programme, project or time period.

- The architect who wants to review the project again now that they have come up with an organizational model for say virtual application delivery.
- The PMO manager who won't let the project into the execution stage because they don't have the "right" project documentation.

All the while the "project" is already burning money in terms of the effort it takes to get through these often conflicting checkpoints[11], already getting late in its delivery, with a solution that's already gradually but inexorably moving towards obsoletion in terms of its chance of achieving the business objectives or keeping pace with technology changes.

Further, we aren't mature enough to marry these two lifecycles in an elegant way or structure the processes with the flexibility required for different types of projects and system implementations, upgrades, modifications, and developments. We are still squeezing every type of system and project through one and only one SDLC and PLC.

If I place office political pressures, personality influences, hidden agendas, petty mindedness, "oopsies," negligence, and even incompetence into the mix, it looks like the diagram on page 182.

---

11 Don't get me wrong, the checkpoints themselves are a good thing in terms of rigor, it's the tangle of nonintegrated processes I'm commenting on here.

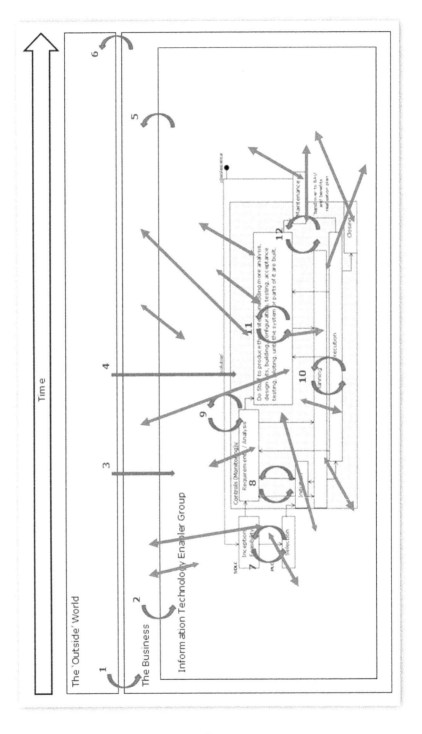

While the diagram is perhaps a flippant way to make a point, the point is never the less valid. IT Project managers will spend as much effort—if not more—dealing with these particular winds of change, rushing backwards and forwards in the direction of the new arrows as they will with managing and trying to cope with legitimate change points.

We all know that there is an ongoing war between the forces of good and the forces of evil. One of the main campaigns of this war manifests itself as the battles between order and chaos. In our organisations and their IT projects this struggle presents itself as the battle between good business process (including IT and project processes in this sense) and "arbitrary" decisions and actions, and bad process (which also produces chaos).

We cannot feasibly provide PMs with any formal methodology to manage what is essentially illogical and cannot be managed by logic (order or process). This type of change will rip through good processes. All the accepted project process and practice in the world is effectively useless when manager or executive xyz, who is higher up in the food chain, makes a play or decision which conflicts with our project management practice. Yes, in theory, this is what governance structures and process is for, but reality warns us to be prepared for a completely arbitrary (in terms of adherence to process) and seemingly random power play, from time to time; or even the completely bizarre and irrational decisions made by people struggling in their jobs.

The only thing that can be done is to point out that this "type of change" is prevalent and needs to be managed to successfully deliver IT projects. There are some rules of thumb to cope with this phenomenon (along with commonly accepted practice) that can protect the project manager and the project:

1. Always get every decision in writing.
2. If someone refuses to put it in writing, this is an indication that something is afoot; hiding is occurring and blaming may follow, it's perhaps time to look for something else somewhere else, but it's definitely time to do a round of project management hygiene practice and make sure our end of things is in shape.
3. In consideration of one and two above, maintain a decision register and implement decision papers as part of your project change control structure and processes.
4. Always maintain a position where your decisions and project position is transparent and defendable—sorry you will just have to always be on top of your game in IT project management.
5. Keep in mind that keeping things like decisions transparent and documented will put you in the firing line and may land you into trouble in a very unhealthy environment, as it will call out or force the hand of the culprits making the environment unhealthy in the first place.

If I was to give a piece of informal advice to new project managers it would be this: at all times stay frosty, not everyone plays by the rules and sometimes it will seem that hardly anyone is.

Projects As Standards, Practices, and Practitioners

It is important to note that this section has been largely rewritten and refocused from the version that went to review, for several important reasons.

Mainly that one of my reviewers pointed out that the first version of this section—focused around a comparison of these standards—actually did the opposite of what I set out to do, and ended up compounding the myths around these standards. I hadn't set out to provide comparisons of these things—just commentaries about the reality of practices—despite the standards—so something had gone wrong somewhere.

Also one of the comments back from a review indicated that more senior practitioners would likely disagree with some of my comments—and not the least what I had said about these standards, programme managers and PMOs—which got me thinking.

In any given engagement over the last few years it seems like I've been the most experienced practitioner around—across the project management standards and all levels of the "project management" space—this isn't a boast, it's not a good thing—it's an abject statement of lack for the IT industry. Where the sheer tidal wave of confusion and misunderstanding of the concepts covered in this section affects those of us in the middle of it, until even our definition of PM standards, roles and functions, and expectations that go with them blur into bad practice as well.

This is how I ended up writing almost the complete opposite of what I had intended in the first version of this section, propounding the whiney "it's too hard" messages and "pick one over another" non-sense, which themselves provide safe harbor for bad practices and bad behaviors—I'd lost my way, again.

There are entire and vast sectors of the IT project landscape where good, intelligent, technically capable people have no idea about the basic nature of a project, why it needs to be handled differently, or that there is a common and international standard related to doing project management correctly. If senior practitioners talked with many of the people in these areas and said the word "programme manager," I suggest their understanding would be drastically differ-ent to the practitioners. Their expectations of a programme man-ager would be the line manager responsible for managing a group of project managers—grouped only by customer account and/or technology implementation. This translates into a hierarchical line authority position who's only skills are to expect that project manag-ers under them know how to run their projects without coordina-tion, to yell at them when this isn't being done, and to finally abuse their formal authoritative position when escalation is needed. This is done outside of established or accepted escalation paths (if these exist) to bang the wrong heads so that they themselves don't get their arse kicked when things go wrong—and always at the project managers' expense. This is why I have used inverted commas around the name programme manager in this book.

None of the higher level and integrative areas in to strategy, align-ments, benefits realization or optimization regarding opportunities would be part of the expectations of a programme manager—with no one in the programme practicing project management as defined in the "standards" body of literature—so that coordination at a pro-ject level within the programme is also not being handled. Further, although these "programme managers" more fit the shape of what we would expect from a project director because the sheer majority have no background in project management, a practitioner's expectation of what should be occurring in project direction is not occurring either.

Recently I reviewed a CV with the title ICT Programme Manager—the owner of which had never actually been in the project space in their entire career.

It's got to the point for me where largely, if there's a "programme manager" involved, it just means extra work and additional stress and effort to go around behind them and fix what they are breaking as they employ no practice in fulfilling their role and don't really understand how it is they are meant to be interacting with the business and the projects "under" them.

As for a senior project manager? Please, this is most likely the layperson who has been in a position the longest—not someone who has grown into the position via an ongoing commitment to developing their practice, coupled with a rich experience of larger and/or more complex projects, and demonstrable outstanding performance on them.

Delivery, practice, and process functions are confused, immature, and change monthly in most PMOs. This is uncontrolled change by people who aren't really sure what they are meant to be doing, or aware that there are standards—not change expected with the evolution of a PMO, as the needs of organsitation and portfolio, programmes, and projects dictate—establishing processes (and I choose my words carefully here—if you would like to picture me bashing your head against practice manuals after each word—go ahead) not remotely related to portfolio, programme, or project management.

While I agree, something is better than nothing, it all goes horribly wrong when that's where it ends, because there is no understanding of PMO evolution, the need for it, the tiers of "project management" or the need to establish processes that actually relate to them—and it is going horribly wrong remember! These PMOs are not on the PMO maturity curve because a) this suggests there will be some movement along it and b) these PMOs do not practically reflect the concept, or demonstrate management of the functions, of a PMO that an experienced practitioner would be familiar with—they are simply another management area in line management.

To make it very clear as we head into this section on standards, in the sense of not taking into account standards and practices that are commonly available and accepted as useful in successful "project management," if you are "making it up" as you go—you are doing it wrong. This is a bad thing. This is what standards are for. I'm saying this because it is clearly evident by the sheer number of IT project failures, that the time for gently supporting organisations in finding their own ways to project management success is over—it is time to prescribe, to get black and white, to up our own games as practitioners in the project management "profession," and be accountable for that.

This area irks me largely because I end up having to not only clean up after the people in the roles above, but also to undertake the roles myself, as well as rescuing the normally top priority, important, complex and engulfed in flames project(s), all at the same time—without charging for it. Practice books are expensive (that's right we should be using them as active references),[12] my time outside of "work" is valuable, but to protect my own and my client's interests on any given engagement, I wear these costs of time and money—researching the best practices and applying them to the situation—to ensure my career isn't damaged and the client gets good results.

---

12 On any given engagement I usually have at least three practice manuals in my work satchel—no really—at present that's PMI's guides on portfolio and programme management, and ISO21500. I'm not a nerd or swat—it's a necessity.

So sit back and relax as we head into the new and improved section on project management standards, now with guidance from the reviewers.

Standards and Other Things

With wild abandon and quite some passion we frequently throw around words like framework and methodology as if they were Ninja throwing stars, with the intention of embedding them cruelly into our colleagues and organisations.

Sometimes, like some Ninja Master from a cheesy Samurai movie, we include the words project, programme, portfolio, PMBOK, PRINCE2, SCRUM and others in our attack; hurling them madly towards our target in rapid succession—as if to overwhelm them by our Zen-like level of PM dexterity and skill; but in seemingly arbitrary orders, and without real thought of whereabouts they will land— or what it is we are saying. Then we grimace as everyone runs for cover, pot plants get knocked over, glass is broken, innocent small fury animals are pinned to the wall, and as the exec/board member nearest our outburst pulls the latest "PRINCE2 framework for SCRUM portfolio management" shuriken we came up with out of their forehead...as we claim its agile project management.

I've included a section on standards in this book for two reasons. One so that it may prompt their appropriate and actual application— which let's face it would be a novel thing—and also so that the next time someone tells me they have set up a PRINCE2 framework or is using "the PMBOK methodology," I can point them to this portion of the book and not use the nearest bendy, rope-like, object to strangle them.

I need to stress again that opinions in this section are mine and definitely not necessarily the opinion of the organizations with which I hold my project management qualifications or those practitioners who have contributed to the reviewed section—especially the throwing star analogy and the bit about small fury animals.[13]

First, let's outline these things called standards.

A Brief, Yet Concise, Explanation of All Those Project Management Standards, Frameworks and Methodologies

The title and content included in this section were permitted by a project management colleague I hold in great esteem, Sean Whitaker. It's from his blog at www.seanwhitaker.com. It is the most concise breakdown and positioning of all the standards I have seen to date.

Sean writes: Are you a little confused by all these project management documents and credentials you keep stumbling across in your quest to understand the profession and further develop yourself as a project manager? Well I'm going to try and explain the situation to you so you understand exactly what a standard, framework and methodology is and how they are different from each other. This will be a brief, yet concise, explanation, and if you want more detail just do a search on the Internet.

Let's start the explanation with a diagram. The diagram shows standards, frameworks, and methodologies in descending order of influence and importance.

---

13 No small fury animals were hurt or injured in the writing of this book—just saying.

```
┌─────────────────────────────────────┐
│  International Standards:            │
│                                     │
│  ISO21500: Guidance on Project      │
│           Management                │
└─────────────────────────────────────┘
                 ▼
┌─────────────────────────────────────┐
│  Frameworks:                        │
│                                     │
│  PMI PMBOK® Guide,                  │
│  APM Body of Knowledge              │
└─────────────────────────────────────┘
                 ▼
┌─────────────────────────────────────┐
│  Methodologies:                     │
│                                     │
│  Method123, TenStep, Scrum, UPMM,   │
│  Prism, Prince2, Lean, XP, Waterfall etc. │
└─────────────────────────────────────┘
```

At the top, you have ISO21500, which is the newly introduced international standard for project management. It took seven years to develop and involved all the project management organizations around the globe and as such represents a truly comprehensive, standardising and unifying approach to project management. It is still early days for this standard, as it was only released in 2012, and as such it is a guiding standard only and not a normative one. We expect it to become a normative standard sometime in the next five years, and when it does, you can start certifying your organisation as ISO21500 compliant. Until then it represents a fantastic guide for professional project management and you should probably make yourself very familiar with it as it will probably become standard you need to comply with sooner or later.

The next layer down is made up of framework documents and their associated credentials. Here you have project management body of knowledge's that capture what is considered good professional project management practice across the entire project management profession. The largest example of this is the PMBOK® Guide from the Project Management Institute (PMI), which is a global organization. Frameworks contain much more detailed information about project management processes, tools, and techniques than standards such as ISO21500. The Association for Project Management (APM), which is largely based in Europe, also has its own body of knowledge as well. Despite this extra information, they do not present specifics ways of completing projects—that's a job for methodologies that we cover soon. There are many similarities between the PMBOK® Guide, APM BoK, and ISO21500, but also a few differences mainly around slight naming and content differences of some processes and process groups. We would expect these differences to be ironed out over the next few years. PMI offers the Project Management Professional (PMP®) and Certified Associate in Project Management (CAPM®) credential, and APM offers its own four-stage certification for project managers. All of these are framework credentials and are at a much more senior and detailed level than methodology credentials which we cover next. I recommend all project managers plan on gaining a framework credential at some point in their career—the sooner the better.

At the bottom of the hierarchy are specific project management methodologies developed from frameworks that, in turn, align with standards. Each methodology can be traced back to a particular framework document, and its ancillary documents such as extensions to the PMI PMBOK® Guide. Each methodology is particularly suitable for different projects based on industry, size, value, complexity, and risk. For example, Scrum is great for fast-moving iterative IT projects, Prince2 for low-complexity IT projects, and Method123 for defined, complex projects from a range of industries. There are usually no, or very little, prerequisites needed to gain a methodology certification so they are generally not any guide to a project managers experience, ability or seniority. My opinion is that

3. PRACTICE MAKES PERFECT

you should only look at becoming a certified in a particular project management methodology if your organization is actually going to use that methodology appropriately. Otherwise I strongly suggest getting a framework credential such as PMP® and gain the skills needed to develop your own project management methodology.

The Voice from the Shadows

That's it; there's nothing more or less to it. It's not confusing, and it's not hard to understand. We have an international standard, which while new, is "the" international standard for project management, two frameworks which cover everything project management in more detail, from different perspectives, but don't prescribe method, and a raft of methodologies at the bottom which specify how to apply project management practices when in particular situations— in-line with the frameworks, while adhering to the single standard.

First thing to note then is that there is, in fact, no ongoing war between the associated project management camps, or drastic conflict between or at the associated levels—so let's stop trying to start one at our level. Many practitioners from every camp have put a great deal of mostly voluntary effort into forming up this total best practice repository of knowledge, based on years of experience in project management and other industries—including IT—which is by the way why it irks me so much when people diss these standards and frameworks, 1) knowledgeable and experienced people have put their own valuable time into helping the idiots who diss them run successful projects and 2) it represents the collection of the best knowledge on the planet about project management—do we really think we know better?!

So the next time we hear someone saying something like "PRINCE2 is better than PMBOK" or "we're only [SCRUM or PRINCE2 or add methodology here],"[14] we will know instantly that the person saying

---

14 I've used these examples as they are the most common I hear in the IT industry, second only to "we stopped using PMBOK and now only use SCRUM."

it doesn't really have an idea what it is they are talking about and little to no grasp on the related subject area they are making such bold claims about. Or that they have completely missed out some important caveats to their statement that would seat what they were saying into their organizational context.

I would so like to go through what Sean has written and make comments regarding the seeming idiocy I have seen in the real world related to the areas described above. So much of what he writes supports many of the points I'm making in this book. But what would be the point? It would make me feel better but wouldn't really be constructive.

Well, OK, maybe a couple of comments then.

Knowing What's What

So "descending order of influence and importance" and "Each methodology can be traced back to a particular framework document, and its ancillary documents"—nicely put.

How about we stop playing methodology buzzword bingo and have conversations about methodologies in the sense of our organisations and types of projects we handle in them. Discussing the need to, in many cases, adopt more than one methodology? Stop using them in name only as technocratic, social, and psychological leverage in our political maneuverings within our organisations? How about we include the standard and a framework in our conversations, and the fit of both the methods to those things *and* our organizational and project management needs? In this sense, applying ISO21500 as a fallback position to use if a method isn't working—yes we need to be able to gauge whether or not a method is working for our projects—to reacquaint ourselves concisely with the patterning of *how* project management should be done in principle; and treating the frameworks as our reservoir of standardized and proven techniques and a more detailed guide to the general progression through a project?

Knowing how to do these things helps you shape (tailor) the right method to your particular present and future needs. Those of us calling ourselves senior project managers, project directors, or anybody senior enough to shape PMOs or approaches to projects for organisations, need to understand the process of identifying when to use specific project management methods. As mentioned before, in IT we also need to be well versed and experienced in identifying and fitting the "shape" of the resulting project to the system lifecycles of the products or technologies—and associated technical practices—in question.

For example, for a simple project, in relatively stable (total) environment, like a print infrastructure roll out to an averagely mature medium sized organisation that is not experiencing too much growth, I'd say use PRINCE2 as the management method and progress the technical stages using waterfall. Why? The rate of change around requirements is likely to be little to none, so it will most likely not matter if some months pass from requirements gathering and sign off (yes, you still have to do this), to the point where the solution is handed over to operations (the length of the project in other words).

If you're developing software of any type, or projects or their products are very complex for any reason (but especially technical reasons) to keep pace with the business and its customers changing their minds (read changing requirements—which again is their prerogative—we IT folk work for the business, not the other way around), make the cultural leap and employ a highly iterative method of *product* development management like SCRUM—with a more intuitive way of specifying requirements—and use SCRUM with a more agile approach to the project and related initiative (acknowledge that a mansion is required, but minimise the risk against change and complexity by focusing on, investing in and building a cottage first, then a house, then maybe a wing extension, then if the business still want it, complete the mansion).

And where is agile project management in all this? To me it is best broadly described as a way of doing project management, which prescribes a flexible and graceful arching approach across the standard and frameworks. Along its arc it grabs the project management principles of iteration, quality, human resource management, and (a focus on) product delivery, and applies them as the principle project management drivers—but not at the expense of the other project management principles. As such and as a result it minimizes overall delivery risk while maximizing delivery success, by—at many project levels—biting off and delivering smaller rationalized and complete chunks of the project products at a time, while holistically acknowledging and handling the iterations and relationships between them—and when complex products are involved, this is why agile project management and SCRUM are used together—the iterative product development method nestles itself within the broader agile project management approach. [15]

So agile project management is not separate to the standard and frameworks either, nor does it conflict in any way with them, but just a note about methodologies for a second—and a reason and caution about blindly adopting them without applying reason.

The methodologies, while fitting within the frameworks and standards, are not always complete project management methods, covering all areas of project management as unfolds in the standard and frameworks.

SCRUM for instance is not a complete project management methodology. It has never been sold as this and in fact the latest SCRUM

---

15 As complete as the customer will accept in many cases—hence the focus of product increment in the latest SCRUM guide, rather than the old "potentially shippable product."

guide specifically states what this thing called SCRUM is—a "process framework."[16] So you won't find a section on contract development or procurement in SCRUM, or guidance on project selection, ties to strategy, or financial management—like you will in ISO21500 and the PMBOK® Guide and extensions. So yet again, as a more senior project manager, we need to know and understand what it is we are dealing with when it comes to our standard, frameworks, and methodologies. However, if implemented within an overall project management approach, SCRUM is a powerful method of delivering complex products.

A few years back, a company of mine was working with a gaming company using SCRUM, producing music for their console games. Because music is a "complex product," I structured the music development process into small, definable, and easily manageable "chunks"; which built upon previous iterations and which we ensured lent themselves to clear acceptance criteria and completeness given the level of acceptance required for each "chunk." This meant we were able to logistically and culturally "sprint" alongside game development with the other "development" teams. This was so successful that we were able to complete a soundtrack for a trailer before the trailer was completed, or even had the final timing for the main sequence confirmed, using only the defined acceptance criteria, a whiteboard storybook, some concept art, and a couple of musical analogues as a guide.[17]

---

16 I'm not quite sure what a process framework is either, I thought SCRUM was a methodology, but I get why the SCRUM guys and gals have made the distinction in the new version of the guide. This is part of their maturity curve and is an acknowledgement that there are many "ways" of doing SCRUM within the SCRUM "way." This distinction of "process framework" confirms that what they are in fact supplying is a framework which if applied in reality, will describe a method of doing things—but other people could apply the process framework slightly differently, still adhering to SCRUM guidelines, but describe a different method.

17 Running all the product component development teams this way also boosted morale along the way. We all used each other's (developmental) outputs for inspiration. Our team used the concept art, visuals, and short animation clips; the artists and developers listened to our sound bites and musical sketches.

Those in the gaming industry may appreciate that this is a significant accomplishment more than those that aren't, but suffice to say that the envelope for this success was created only because of a successful adaptation of SCRUM.

Who Have We Just Hired?

"There are usually no, or very little, prerequisites needed to gain a methodology certification so they are generally not any guide to a project managers experience, ability or seniority."

Man, think I'll just let that sentence speak for itself. Just leave it there and let it all soak in, as the statement basks in all its black and white glory.

I have already had a rant about this in the application of practice section, so here really all we need to do is let it sink in.

Wow, so what we are saying here is that we better check carefully before leaving someone who is only PRINCE2 certified or only a certified SCRUM master in charge of large swags of our IT project landscapes—or even a project; or placing them in an organisation that runs projects by a different method? That, by the sounds of it, *anyone* can attend these courses and attain these credentials? That merely attaining this level of credential doesn't actually equate or always attest to the quality or capability of a person as a project manager?

You see once again it's not a problem with the credentials or methodologies themselves, far from it—and once again for the record a good and considered application of PRINCE2 and SCRUM will produce success in our IT projects. Nor is it an issue to do with those scrum masters and PRINCE2 practitioners who are experienced in project management and the application of these methods—watching these credential holders execute their projects within their method puts my generally lazy and "would rather be sleeping" attitude to life to shame!

It's yet again an issue with the lackaday and complacent way we hire, manage, and generally go about our bullying, self-obsessed, self-motivated "office administration" and "chuck mud at it until it sticks" approaches to project management in general, where our focus is anything but project management.

It's time to ask ourselves who has our PMO or programme manager just hired? Why are they hiring them? Are those managers themselves in the same category? Or do they have the experience, peer and mentoring support, aptitude, and qualifications that people in their position actually need to have? Are they themselves actually undertaking personal on-going development in the project management space? What are they actually doing? Sssssssh! They're coming, they'll hear us!

Is there a little thought in the back of your mind while reading this, scratching and scrabbling around the equation of the IT project management space you work in, and the correlation to the failures that keep occurring in them? Can you hear it yet? Did you or someone you know just hire someone from IT operations into a project management related position? Did we send a developer off on a PRINCE2 course because we need them to run that project coming up—expecting them to "be a project manager" when they get back?

In many situations this area of IT project management really is a case of the blind leading the blind—right up through to the exec level. I'll say it again, just because we need someone to be a project manager doesn't make them one. One irony here is that very early on in my project management career people said to me that I wasn't a really project manager—and—begrudgingly perhaps—they were right—at the time.

Another irony, of course, is that this is all very easily fixed if we just make ourselves familiar with the "standards" and many of the organisations behind the frameworks and methodologies actually openly offer assistance to anyone who seriously asks for it.

What a Friend we have in ISO21500

To be fair—and I'll give you this one—I am a sad person that needs to get out more, because it was a very happy day for me when ISO21500 Guidance on Project Management was released in 2012, and I was more excited than anyone should probably be when the copy I ordered came in the post.[18]

The reasons for this is that what I think IT project management and the project management industry in general has been missing, is that single point of reference, that "we can all hang our hats on this one" kind of guidance that—as the problems covered in this book make clear—is sorely needed in this "profession."

And that's another good thing about ISO21500; it's a step towards standardizing project management that will ultimately result in the creation of the profession of project management. A place where vagaries and problems stemming from nonprescription, lack of understanding, political turbulence, multiple seemingly conflicting camps, and incapability can be resolved in the light of accepted truth. If I'm lucky this will happen in my professional lifetime.

We can't argue with what's in ISO21500—well, we can, but generally speaking it's a unifying "best of breed." Unless we have come up with a new and better way of shaping and managing projects, arguments against ISO21500 will be hollow, lacking substance, and will point to the real motivatations of those who are arguing.

It's perhaps the beginning of the end of so much of the nonsense in around IT project management, the catalyst that will force IT PMOs and practitioners, and the organisations they exist within, to make a

---

18   As sad as this is, I do promise to get out more and interact with real people when I've finished this book.

concerted and considered effort to align all practice in this area—at the very least as an arse-covering exercise, if nothing else, when it becomes normative; and currently it's light, concise, and easy to understand.

So much so, that I was surprised when my copy of ISO21500 arrived in the post.

I was expecting another tome of material like OCG and PMI produce with their manuals—which is always cool to get. At first I was a little disappointed, but as I thumbed through the headings and diagrams, it was all there, in its entire concise thirty-six- pages, well-worded in plain language, glory. It placed project management within the context of the organization. It provided an easily understandable breakdown of governance and covered projects from their embry-onic beginnings to their closing activities. The representation of a project was structured like it is in the PMBOK® Guide, yet its con-cepts worded in similar fashion to how the APM BoK expresses these concepts.

All I could think was—wow, awesome, and well done. Just have a think before you diss or ignore this standard and associated frame-work and methodologies, some very clever people have done some very clever things in ISO21500, on behalf and for all of us.

It's so good that, and I use my words carefully here, I have armed myself with this standard, almost literally. I've loaded it into my abstraction of all things project management to use in my "first run through" any project related review or engagement—have these people got the basics right?

So this is the only recommendation in terms of our combined "standards" I will make in this book. I know money may be tight, but if you're intending to make a "profession" of project management, or have a real need to understand project management, then I strongly recommend spending the $180ish dollars and buying a copy of this document, and becoming intimately familiar with it.

To everyone who had anything remotely to do with forming ISO21500—good job!

ES IST KINDER-GARTEN NICHT: CONCLUSION

Ich will eure Stimmen hoeren
Ich will die Ruhe stoehren
Ich will das ihr mich gut seht
Ich will das ihr mich versteht..

Seht ihr mich
Versteht ihr mich
Fühlt ihr mich
Hoert ihr mich
Rammstein: Ich Will

So, where have we gotten to? From my point of view, I've been polite and restrained, and supportive where I can be. I've tried my best not to revert to accusatory language and expletives, yet I now feel the whole book lacks the level of "Oh my God, you can't be serious!" punch it was intended to pack. I still feel the need to get the point across as concisely as possible.

In summary, because of a mix of inexperience, a lack of skills, a lack of understanding, and, in some instances, capability—and coupled with social and political influences, bad behaviours, and sometimes seeming idiocy, across all levels of our organisations—our IT projects are failing.

They do not fail because we failed to engage with stakeholders properly or didn't work out an appropriate ROI or treatment for the business case. Nor did they fail because our resources were over-burdened, because we developed a project schedule that was too detailed or not detailed enough. They are also not failing because we had ineffective selection and initiation processes, because we didn't get a sound footing "in the business" for the project, because requirements or scopes were unclear or nonexistent, or because our PMO processes had little if anything to do with project man-agement. All of these things are the results of what I've outlined in this book.

IT project management needs to be a professionally applied practice. It requires an in-depth understanding of the principles of project management and nature of projects themselves—with an associ-ated applied management of those understandings. IT requires an active and supportive peer network and mentoring structure. It's not "office administration" that "anyone can do," and it fails when taking the associated "chuck mud at it until it sticks" approach. It takes professionally skilled resources to manage and complete an IT project, and those resources must also have a good background in IT practices and a technical grounding.

Successful IT project management and IT projects require high-performance resources that can perform consistently and continu-ally in (relatively) short, highly pressured, bursts of brilliance, con-strained by and mindful of short timeframes, tight budgets, and delivering to specific and defined outputs who can work and stick to an agreed "plan"—so they also need to understand the nature of projects. IT projects should not be filled from those of the 9–5 "living dead" persuasion, without the motivation, skills, experience, or knowledge—or support—to perform in the dynamic manner required; nor should they be filled with the political alligators that infest the social waterways of the pseudo-democracies we call our organisations.

The IT project environment is also the complete opposite of the cuddly, fluffy, PC world of HR in everyday business activity. It is a task and results orientated environment, where good "people management" is the result of transparent, honest, and demonstrably culpable leadership. "Line" management and support processes cannot be applied to the project environment. People will get their "fingers caught between the bricks" of project delivery failure if we adopt a "lovey dovey," consultative and gentle approach to HR management in our IT projects. That approach fails to protect our resources from the immediate, pressured, and total accountability that occurs when project delivery failures are experienced; there is no "next financial period" in which to sweep the result of poor practice and performance to "soften the blows."

The approach to supportive HR management for IT projects is best summed up with a quote by Nigel Powers, "If you've got an issue, here's a tissue.," Otherwise you need to become part of a solution—at least there's a tissue on offer here! Literally the very people that may be offended by this attitude—and lack the understanding that it comes with more respect for and commitment to individuals assigned to projects and their success—are the very people that should be prevented from operating in IT project environments.

Est ist kindergarten nicht - the IT project world is not kindergarten.

To reiterate, IT project failures are costing organisations millions upon millions of dollars and pounds. In some situations, basic project management practice and the understanding of projects is so poor and the environment so politically turbulent that basic project management practices cannot actually be implemented. In other situations the environments are so unhealthy that implementation of basic project management practice actually "shows up" those "in charge" or that are "hiding something" and ultimately lands the project manager in hot water—and in particularly toxic environments, ironically, gets the project manager labeled as a "bad project manager." In this sense the IT project management environment as a whole is caustic and extraordinarily damaging to the careers of those "professional" PMs who work within it.

Remember this isn't just my message, the consultants, programme and project managers, and techs that were kind enough to be candid with me when researching this book, enabled me to construct the following sentence from their words about what they felt about project management in IT (my ever-optimistic words in square brackets): "[The present level of] project management related practice in IT is abjectly and prolifically atrocious."

Further, when I asked what makes a good project manager, the answer always came in two parts. Half the answer was always the same "A good grasp of project basics" (lifecycles, structures, techniques, and practices)—sometimes this was expressed as a "goes without saying" attitude—which I gently pointed out actually needs saying. The other responses were diverse, personality based, and not remotely related to any professional practice at all—which is a principal reason for the extent of social commentary in this book. Here's a summarized list of the responses, and let's start with my favorite first.

What makes a good project manager?

- Applied personality
- Endurance, tenacity and a thick skin
- Pragmatism—the application of common sense
- A Self-starter/go getter
- A high EQ and IQ
- Honesty, openness, integrity
- Insanity

I think the first comment summarizes the rest neatly, applied personality, a social force to be reckoned with; just consider this list as a whole for a second.

Excuse the philosophical digression, but we seem to be holding the project manager to some sort of myth and applying that myth in our professional lives. The qualities ascribed to good project managers are nothing short of those very qualities ascribed to heroes in myth throughout the ages, like Job, Homer, Thor, and Frodo for that matter. If this is the case, and no matter if it's accurate for any given individual PM—good luck with that, it's no wonder good PMs upset so many people. Anyone holding this myth somewhere in their subconsciousness, along with any level of inferiority complex, will be threatened by a PM with half a dose of the qualities above—more so for a PM who also has a strong grasp of the nature of projects and their management practices and the ability to apply them.

This is why I think project managers have become the pariahs of the IT project world. It's that basic human nature to worship certain human beings as heroes, to offload life responsibilities on to them, to hold them up to the highest standards, and to turn around when they crumble under the pressure or start making so much sense that they threaten change on their worshipers—and especially if they are speaking a different language ("projectese" in this sense)—and nail the poor bastards to the nearest cross, exile them, or label them as heretics and stone them—which is the most accurate descriptive analogy in this book for so many of the IT project review, status, and board meetings I have had the misfortune to attend in the last ten years.

When I ask, "What's happening in IT project management?" I'm not just spitting the words out rhetorically; I really am asking the question. The answer—that the technologies are evolving professional environments so quickly that the roles and the abilities and capabilities needed of them are changing rapidly; yet the attitudes and acumen,

ES IST KINDERGARTEN NICHT

both socially and professionally, constrained by the law of average, are not evolving with them—is of absolutely no use to us at present.

This is because, and I have tried to avoid using that hackneyed "bingo word" paradigm so far in this book, we seem to be in the middle of a massive change. The relatively recent advent of the memeplex[19] of the project manager, projects, and IT itself is new and forming. We haven't even completed a generation since IT really got up front and nasty in the face of business. Why are we surprised that this heroic myth and the successful actions that are expected of it is having trouble seating itself in a society that acknowledges the related problems only via something as cuttingly satirical as *Office Space*, *The Office*, and Dilbert? This seems to be doing its damnedest to throw every spanner into the works it possibly can to prevent IT project managers and IT projects from succeeding.

To get back on the project management track, good IT project managers everywhere—beware! You are carrying a huge social load because of the lack of understanding of what you are, what you do and need to do, how you need to do it, how this differs from everyday activity, and what support you need to do it. In every engagement you are walking into a level of this societal phenomenon.

For me, I see this all stretching out in front of me with every new organisation and every new contract. Good people, generally capable people, and unhappy people not acting that great are having a bad time in the field of IT project management and causing IT projects to fail. They are causing IT projects to fail because they aren't sure what their jobs are and know something is missing from their practice of project management. They cannot do anything about this because they do not have the required qualifications, skills, and experience to actually fulfill their roles.

---

19 And then to immediately use another bingo buzzword.

This isn't a criticism of the people; it's a criticism against our current practices—practices that halo those into rolls that shouldn't really be in them and who then hire more of the same because they can't identify what skills and experience is really needed. These practices support and encourage people with a penchant for megalomania, empire building, covering their arse, and other bad behaviors; and the senior executive management which enable this to continue for the same reasons.

To be even more frank for a second, in the last few years I've had the central business district of the city I had lived in all my life raised by an earthquake, taking with it the IT PM contract market, a close and pivotal family member die of cancer, moved cities and "started again," more upheaval professionally and personally because of these things than I have had in my entire life—and still shaped, recovered or delivered successfully millions of dollars worth of IT programme and projects—despite having to deal with the things outlined in this book—and then written this book—all in the same period.

Successful IT project management can be done even in the most trying of circumstances if only the basic practices are followed—and if I can go through all of this and achieve these things, is it really a surprise that I'm no longer prepared to just sit smiling inanely and nodding as the people around me, yet again, clumsily and completely destroy IT projects because of the reasons outlined in this book?

I was actually advised by a colleague when writing this book not to worry about this so much and "work half as hard and just take the money." Really? That's your answer? Just go along with the flow and rip off my employers?

In summation,[20] personally I'm left a little conflicted. On the one hand, if I could earn the same or better salary making music, mov-

---

20   And it's Sum-mation not Sarmatian—the Sarmatians were an ancient Scythian (Iranian) people that lived between the fourth and fifth centuries BC, well known for their immense dislike of IT project management failures.

ies and games, I would probably never take on another IT project management role on in my life. On the other hand, I still love IT and project management, and the people I work alongside, and the fulfillment that is achieved when *we* deliver something successfully...but come on people we really do suck at this.

www.ingramcontent.com/pod-product-compliance
Lightning Source LLC
Chambersburg PA
CBHW070943050326
40689CB00014B/3320